SO HELP ME GOD
Religion and the Presidency,
Wilson to Nixon

. . . I WILL FAITHFULLY EXECUTE THE OFFICE

OF PRESIDENT OF THE UNITED STATES, AND WILL

TO THE BEST OF MY ABILITY, PRESERVE, PROTECT

AND DEFEND THE CONSTITUTION OF THE UNITED

STATES.

SO HELP ME GOD
Religion and the Presidency, Wilson to Nixon

by Robert S. Alley

 **JOHN KNOX PRESS**
Richmond, Virginia

Library of Congress Cataloging in Publication Data

Alley, Robert S.   1932–
    So help me God: religion and the Presidency.

    Includes bibliographical references.
    1. Presidents—U. S.—Religion.   2. Nationalism
and religion—U. S.   3. Messianism, American.
I. Title.
BR516.A7   261.7   70–37418
ISBN 0–8042–1045–4

To my father

REUBEN EDWARD ALLEY

Who taught me about freedom and justice

"Leaving Religion To Private Initiative
Is Un-American!"

From *Straight Herblock* (Simon & Schuster, 1964)

Preface

This undertaking, like all human effort, is dependent for its completion upon the encouragement of many friends and colleagues. The idea for the book originated in extended conversations with Dr. William C. Smith, Jr. As the work unfolded, the regular dialogic encounters, often heated, with my associate, Professor Robison B. James, gave clarity and focus to my intentions. Further, I believe that my active participation in political affairs, notably working in the Eugene McCarthy campaign of 1968, convinced me that the "New Politics" was in need of larger historical vision.

In the preparation of the manuscript I owe a real debt to two kind friends. Former Ambassador Murat Williams gave a critical reading to the material and offered extremely helpful suggestions. The other indispensable ingredient has been the skilled insights extended by Robert E. Shepherd, Jr.

For his time and comments on the whole period under consideration I would express an especially warm word of thanks to Professor Eric Goldman of the Department of History at Princeton University. Naturally, none of those persons mentioned is accountable for my interpretations and observations.

Appreciation is also expressed for assistance granted by the University of Richmond Committee on Research.

Every good thing I have done has had a family attachment. My wife, Norma, understands my thoughts, and no man could have greater help than that in the writing task. My parents provided the environment where politics mattered, and every child should be that fortunate. My father has provided invaluable research assistance on the present undertaking. My children reminded me regularly of real priorities which often facilitated meeting deadlines.

Every person should have friends of long years, colleagues who stimulate, and a family that cares. He is doubly blessed if he has also had a Christian minister who spoke the truth. In subtle ways this book is a better product because of Dr. Vernon Britt Richardson, who holds an honored place in the memory of our family.

Contents

If the democratic nations fail, their failure must be partly attributed to the faulty strategy of idealists who have too many illusions when they face realists who have too little conscience.

—REINHOLD NIEBUHR

Most Presidents have a hierarchy of values that is seldom articulated but is discernible in their actions.

—LOUIS W. KOENIG

Caution is the confidential agent of selfishness.
—WOODROW WILSON

Introduction

The study of recent American history causes a progressive person to feel lonely indeed. The momentous events which actually occurred and the dreams of even greater accomplishments that filter through the words of a Wilson or a Franklin Roosevelt may generate a certain nostalgia, for even the dreams seemed somehow realizable then. Yet as one looks back from 1972, over a quarter of a century has passed since the death of FDR, and the dreams are remote indeed. Jonathan Daniels spoke of that era as the "Loss of Innocence," but the hopes still inspired men of goodwill to strive for a "better" world. For many, the period since 1945 has become a time of the "Loss of Hope." Even the youth and vigor of John F. Kennedy could not restore the faded vision, and the words from Camelot sound perhaps merely pathetic when related to him. And as if the sixties would allow not even the last vestige of hope to escape to the seventies, it robbed the nation of Martin Luther King, Jr., and Robert Kennedy. In fact, the roll call of the dead in that decade is startling to those who find assurances in great leadership.

Our attempt at evaluation of religious influences upon the

office of the President of the United States from Wilson to Nixon must cope with this loss of hope, ironically in an age when the latest movement in theology is that of hope. A current volume on the subject of religion and its influence upon national policy, published in 1971, cites no recent documents except those by King and Kennedy and the warning words of Senator J. William Fulbright in the *Arrogance of Power*. The prophetic Senator serves as a reminder of Wilson with his erudition and of Roosevelt with his activism but his challenge to the latter half of the twentieth century is unheeded. Most citizens are just not listening to him. The nation appears leaderless both politically and morally as it turns and shifts in an effort to recover values it does not understand. In most ways President Nixon fills the office presently as an anachronism.

Recently a student asked what it was like to live in the forties with its aspirations and sense of morality. I struggled for words to convey my own feelings and I found it practically impossible to communicate intelligibly. With a sincere desire to bridge that gap this volume is presented. And as we examine whence we have come, we may be constrained to ask whither we as a nation and a people may go.

But you are a fool if in the back of your head you do not know it is possible that you are mistaken.

—WOODROW WILSON

I • What Is Civil Religion?

In the winter of 1967 Robert N. Bellah, Professor of Sociology at the University of California, wrote a scholarly article entitled "Civil Religion in America." It rapidly became a "frame" for several other papers by prominent thinkers who had interest in the same theme. The Bellah thesis received widespread attention, and many thoughtful citizens participated in the ensuing discussion. During the 1969 annual meeting of the American Academy of Religion in Boston, Professor Bellah was honored when an entire section of the program was built around his ideas. Church historian Sidney Mead was active among those who championed Bellah's position. On the other hand, there were dissenters. Professor Sidney Ahlstrom, distinguished church historian from Yale University, firmly declared that Bellah was struggling with a dead issue. In short, reactions have been as varied as they have been numerous to this instructive and documented presentation. The following is Bellah's own summary of his thesis.

While some have argued that Christianity is the national faith, and others that church and synagogue celebrate only the generalized religion of "the American Way of Life," few have realized

that there actually exists alongside of and rather clearly differentiated from the churches an elaborate and well-institutionalized
civil religion in America. This article argues not only that there
is such a thing, but also that this religion—or perhaps better, this
religious dimension—has its own seriousness and integrity and
requires the same care in understanding that any other religion
does.[1]

These ideas are not new, though the term "civil religion"
had not recently been employed to describe the phenomenon.[2]
As early as 1958 Martin E. Marty wrote:

There are four major partners in the religious situation of
today's America. Three of them—Protestants, Catholics, and
Jews—go about their business in relatively peaceful coexistence.
The fourth partner, however, is gaining, and at the expense of
the other three, for he draws his recruits from among their
members. What is more, the "convert" to the fourth partner may
retain his membership in his original community of faith. The
national religion thrives on "plural belonging." It makes fewer
demands on potential converts and operates with an inner logic
that defies massive refutation.[3]

It is doubtful that Bellah can claim with justification that
this "fourth partner" has been "left in obscurity." The evidence
may suggest otherwise, perhaps beginning with H. Richard
Niebuhr. And clearly Marty offered a profound analysis of this
historical reality with the chilling reminder that it "defies massive refutation." Its obscurity may merely be a lack of concern
on the part of professionals and citizens alike. We regularly
witness this "partner" in action.

In the spring of 1964 Billy Graham held a news conference
in Atlantic City. He was in his element, a conference dominated
by congenial religious journalists. He was discussing, with notable enthusiasm, his personal support for a constitutional
amendment to alter the First Amendment in order to allow
Bible reading and organized prayer in the public schools of
America. Mr. Graham waxed eloquent upon the need for moral

influence in our schools and spoke of what he called "non-sectarian" prayer and praise. One reporter asked if he believed that only through the God in Christ could one be assured of eternal salvation. Reacting to the question eagerly and with Bible in hand, Mr. Graham warmed to the leading remark with the affirmation that he certainly did believe that. The second inquiry cooled his ardor only slightly when the reporter asked if Graham thought Jews had to believe in God as defined in the Christian faith in order to be saved. Graham affirmed this. Then he was asked: "How then can you speak of non-sectarian prayer when you affirm there is only one God and he can be known only in Jesus Christ? What God, by your definition, would be equally acceptable to Jew and Christian alike?" Graham was somewhat flustered when he responded with a question, "Do you mean the God up there or the God in Christ?" He became quite aggravated as he dismissed the questioner with obvious displeasure, passing to safer ground with another reporter.[4]

Of course, Graham is not a dualist in his views, he does not believe in two Gods, and he was using a figure that snared him. Nevertheless, he was asserting what amounted to a dualism, which he regularly affirms on occasions when he moves from his "Hour of Decision" to a White House Prayer Breakfast. Billy Graham is only one of many evidences of a burgeoning national cult in the United States.

In an assessment of the validity of any such national cult our two scholars part company. Marty says Protestants "must vigorously rebel against the new establishment, against the official sanctioning of an attitude toward the religion of democracy or realized pluralism in general."[5] To Bellah, on the other hand, "It is in need—as is any living faith—of continual reformation, of being measured by universal standards. But it is not evident that it is incapable of growth and new insight."[6]

Richard Niebuhr in the *Social Sources of Denominationalism* revealed a concern with the problem when he spoke of denominationalism as the evil of the modern church. He suggested that the incipient national cult was no more than the corruption of the Christian faith. The civil religion's whole character is conditioned by more than 350 years of Judeo-Christian influence. Whether one quotes Jefferson or Lincoln, Eisenhower or Kennedy, the presence of that influence is unmistakable. The independent fourth force draws heavily from the religious tradition which Niebuhr describes. Christianity "in its denominational aspect, at least, . . . has become part and parcel of the world, one social institution alongside of many others."[7]

By Niebuhr's yardstick, if this "social institution" has now become a civil religion, it is a bad thing. It reflects the provincialism of religion bound to state chauvinism. The "In God We Trust" mentality is encouraged and may quickly become the very stuff of narrow nationalism. Marty views this as inevitable and dangerous, thus setting the church the task of a prophetic voice against it. Bellah is more optimistic. He looks at a Jefferson, a Lincoln, a Kennedy, and sees hope for genuine reformation toward a "liberal" civil religion. He bases this expectation on the conclusion that in the first instance, "political commitment in the United States contains a prime component of primordial religious commitment."[8] Having, to his satisfaction, established this "fact," he moves to the assumption that what exists can be improved. He believes that this commitment has roots in the principles of justice and freedom espoused by Jefferson and others. In all this, Bellah, like most other analysts of the problem, employs the work of the French sociologist Emil Durkheim, *The Elementary Forms of the Religious Life.*

If, as many have presumed, there is in America a kind of civil religion presently active, a national cult in process, two questions are in order. First, is there some clear-cut guideline by which that religion or cult can be identified and defined? Is a creed for the civil religion possible? We shall return to these considerations shortly. Second, is it possible to make a value judgment concerning that religion respecting its positive or negative effects upon the populace and the religious institutions? Professor Lewis Lipsitz of the University of North Carolina observed: "If, then, there are specific large-scale evidences for the infusion of religious tendencies into American politics, they would probably be most apparent along these two dimensions: Intense and often intolerant patriotism, and implicit reverence for the President, particularly in times of crisis."[9] This led Lipsitz, along with Marty and others, to render a negative assessment of the value of any civil religion.

Returning to our first inquiry, if we assume that there is some type of political religious reality, there are two alternatives for defining the civil religion. On the one hand, the civil religion may be assessed as the normal expectation of a nation state. From that one could deduce that the determination of its character would be through the study of the national "philosophy" of government. This is essentially what Bellah has done. He allows for very little outside of presidential addresses and political documents as the sources for the civil religion creed. And he is highly selective in his interpretation of those items. He arrives thereby at an ideal which he asserts is the American way in civil religion. Allowing his assumptions, he produces an impressive case. But it may be contended that what one sees in the nation is not explained by so precise a historical structure.

On the other hand, it may properly be asserted that the national cult results from the powerful personalities of leaders in a given time, most particularly the Presidents. This would not eliminate the natural proclivity for religious ritual in national affairs, but it would make it less certain that anyone could correctly describe a "true" civil religion from the rites and ceremonies. Civil religion could consequently be bent to good or bad ends, depending upon the personalities involved. Then "intense and often intolerant patriotism" could be used or misused by a President who enjoyed "implicit reverence." In such a case the only objective criterion for the concerned observer would be what may be regarded as the overall national interest, certainly not moral judgments of right and wrong.

If we proceed along this second line, the observable religious state ritual will be construed as a product of particular national figures in their expression of religious attitudes. The thrust of this study is in the direction of an emphasis upon presidential personalities and their religious thoughts. In doing this we shall view civil religion as far more fluid a reality than Professor Bellah would appear to allow. In other words, the national mood, the international balance of power, and the strength of presidential personalities tend to construct a new civil religion in every generation. At the same time, peculiar circumstances leading to our present character as a nation limit political options and that in turn limits the variety of civil religious expressions possible.

By this thesis we shall attempt a thematic study of the role of religion in the civil body politic from 1912 through 1972. How did the various Presidents relate to the international issues and, in a lesser degree, to domestic issues? How did they employ religious motifs, consciously or otherwise, in their solutions? Can a correlation be noted between the changing character of the national cult and the early religious involvement of the persons under examination? Finally, how did the religious communities respond to political issues in relation to the presidency? It might also occur to a perceptive observer to ask whether the sum total of activities of the leaders tended to formalize a fourth religious option in our day. Will such a formulation preclude the election of some types of persons in the future? For even if we may contend today that there is no ritualistic and dogmatic civil religion, this does not argue that there never will be.

Professor John F. Wilson of the Department of Religion

at Princeton University has recently engaged in discussion of the topic of civil religion in a collection *The Religion of the Republic*. He raises the most pertinent question, "Should these phenomena be termed religious?"[10] He concludes, "The elements out of which full-blown common or civil religion could be shaped may be present, but they come together more in terms of diverse elements of piety juxtaposed in a 'culture' than as a formal religion."[11]

In this excellent essay Wilson has struck the major point, a point which supports observations to be made in the concluding chapter to the effect that Bellah has relied too heavily on the Durkheim thesis, ignoring thereby progress from primitive to more complex society. It is to be hoped that the present study of the presidency will focus attention upon diversity and divergence, with concern for history, in order to establish the fact that there is no one civil religion either demanded by our traditions or existing in fact. However, this postulation does not preclude the development of such a civil religion based upon the false reading of the past and the misunderstanding of democracy for the future.

I believe in an America . . . where religious liberty is so indivisible that an act against one church is treated as an act against all.

—JOHN F. KENNEDY

II • Religion and the State Viewed Historically

So many studies have been made of the involvement between church and state during the early years of American history that it would be out of place to attempt to supply extensive treatment of that theme in this work.[1] Nevertheless, though the general outline is reasonably clear, we shall make a brief review of some portions of the story in order to give interpretation.

From the beginning in 1607 the Church of England was firmly established in Virginia and for well over a century that Establishment remained unchallenged. Not until the mid-eighteenth century was any real dissenting voice heard in the first colony. In contrast, dissent within the English church was the cause of the dramatic Plymouth experiment of 1620. However, by 1691 that settlement had been absorbed by the Massachusetts Bay Colony, which had been founded in 1629 by the Puritans who had come to stay and prosper in their "New Israel." By the middle of the following decade Roman Catholics with judicious adjustments had settled in Maryland and the "Left Wing" of the Protestant Reformation had found refuge in Roger Williams' Rhode Island. Thus by 1640 all the warring factions in England that precipitated the Cromwell period were actively involved in the colonial experiment. It is not strange, therefore, that despite the efforts of the "saints" in New England and the clergy in Virginia, it was impossible to bring about a permanent religious establishment for all in America. Though we may see this clearly in retrospect, it was not obvious at all to the men and women who were part of the early struggle. An important fact here is that religious pluralism led to the adoption of a voluntary principle in religious affiliation.[2]

Religious liberty, first espoused by Roger Williams, successfully triumphed later in the new nation under the political leadership of Thomas Jefferson and James Madison. The means of achieving this end was through a provision in the organic law to provide for separation of church and state. All American Presidents from Washington to Nixon have administered under this identical constitutional article relative to religion and the state: "Congress shall make no law respecting an establishment of religion, or prohibiting the free exercise thereof." The presidency did not evolve from a religious establishment with assumptions about God and ruler like those common in European nations. The new nation, born in 1776, formulated something unique. There were no religious traditions to be maintained, only those to be avoided. It is instructive here to read the words of de Tocqueville. "In the United States religion exercises but little influence upon the laws and upon the details of public opinion; but it directs the customs of the community, and, by regulating domestic life, it regulates the state."[3]

Under such an arrangement it was to be expected that strong leadership would find and employ various means of injecting religion into the national life. In spite of the Bill of Rights, it might have gradually taken the form of an establishment of one dominant religious tradition. Alternatively, it might have followed the proposal of Patrick Henry and created a general assessment to support Christianity as the national faith. Or, possibly, it might have developed independently as a distinct force in national history with its own peculiar character and tradition. A fourth alternative is supplied by Bellah and Marty, who claim there is in America a dual loyalty among citizens concerning religion, a dualism that may encourage even a strictly orthodox Christianity to demand prayer in public institutions but at the same time insist that public prayer shall be non-sectarian, in order to avoid offense to political neighbors.

Protestantism in America had passed through at least one major revolution before the founding of the nation in 1776. Beginning around 1720 and lasting until the French and Indian War, the Great Awakening left a permanent impression on the religion of America. In the middle colonies the Tennents, encouraged by the visit of George Whitefield from England and by the large numerical response to his preaching, created a major crisis for Presbyterianism. The liberal intellectuals of that denomination were bested in the evangelical jousting, and the result was the establishment of a "New Side" dominance. These evangelicals had sought to bring vitality to the dormant religious structures of their day. Their triumph preserved Presbyterianism for "orthodoxy," and the "true Christian spirit" was protected from academic "coldness." Calvinism was thereby firmly rooted as an important fruit of the Awakening. Like most religious movements, of course, the Awakening was largely a mirror of the social upheaval of the area during the eighteenth century.

The Awakening seemed equally promising in New England among the Puritans or Congregationalists. They, like the Presbyterians, had been solidly Calvinist. And the champion of the "New Light" group was the dauntless intellectual giant Jonathan Edwards, minister of Northampton, Massachusetts. Unlike the middle colonies, however, there were in New England two centers of higher learning—Harvard and its offspring, Yale. Edwards viewed both institutions with suspicion, they having separated evangelical faith from reason. Harvard president Charles Chauncy was Edward's chief detractor, and in contrast to what had occurred in Pennsylvania and New Jersey, Edwards was finally discredited locally and forced to resign his pulpit. Liberalism won in New England, and Congregationalism became the seedbed of Unitarianism. Jonathan Edwards moved in 1755 to become president of the Presbyterian New Side college, the Log College of New Jersey. Within a century Presbyterians became disenchanted with their academic child, abandoned Princeton University, and established, in the same town, a seminary which became the heartbeat of the orthodox in the latter part of the nineteenth century.

In examining the history of higher education in this country as a creation of American Protestantism, a rather pathetic picture emerges. Most of the fine educational institutions were fostered by the church, but the church failed to understand what it had nurtured; consequently, in their effort to enforce orthodoxy in faith, the denominations fell prey to obscurantism while the schools of their creation demanded independence. Higher education when properly conceived is inherently liberal, the enemy of enforced orthodoxy, the champion of freedom. Failure of the churches to recognize the true nature of education led to tragic divisions between faith and reason.

Prior to the American Revolution, then, two distinct Protestant movements had emerged and a severe alienation of Congregationalism from orthodox Calvinism had developed. The Church of England did not face a serious theological challenge in that period, and the only effect of the Awakening which it felt was membership attrition. As the hostilities of 1776 approached, the Anglican tie with the mother country became a growing embarrassment, particularly since there was no bishop in the colonies. Nevertheless, the link with the Book of Common Prayer remained firm.

From this brief survey we observe that there were three historical religious traditions—Congregational-Unitarian, Calvinist, and Episcopalian—which have continued as vital factors in affecting the political ethics in the national affairs of the United States. For identification purposes we shall label these as types A, B, and C, respectively.

For the United States the rise of any civil religion is directly affected in character and form by the quality of religion exemplified by the President as chief administrator. Any cultic development is essentially a contradiction rather than an affirmation of American heritage, but this does not, for the future, preclude just that kind of thing.

The civil religion about which we have been speaking has a history but no predictable future except as a function of the presidential will. What the future holds for the threefold scheme in the election of Catholics, Jews, or Blacks to the presidency is uncertain. The only non-Protestant thus far has been John Kennedy, a Catholic, who responded as President quite in accord with his predecessors of the Anglican tradition. A fuller consideration of the three types follows.

Type A. Congregationalism, galvanized by the intellectual victory of the eighteenth century, produced a kind of religious thinking that was regularly unorthodox or non-orthodox as measured by Protestant standards. Members of this group equated religion with morality, and morality was for them essentially the product of human reason. Therefore, political ethics came to be the outgrowth of enlightened humanism. While these citizens were not particularly concerned to deny that their roots were in traditional Christianity, they vigorously repudiated the restrictive proclivities of the church and its creeds. In the early days of the Republic, Presidents Adams, Jefferson, and Madison had projected their administrations according to this line of thought. The effect was to encase the First Amendment in the mold of separationism. In fact, Jefferson and Madison were chief architects of the separationist philosophy. It seems evident that if a civil religion had manifested itself in those early days it would of necessity have had to be distinct from the orthodox patterns of the various sects and denominations.

Along with Lincoln these early Presidents became models for Bellah's thesis. In associating the modern civil religion with the two great Americans, he says, "Still, it has been difficult to use the words of Jefferson and Lincoln to support special interests and undermine personal freedom."[4] Bellah is correct that neither Lincoln nor Jefferson saw national cultic acts as substitutes for the traditional sectarian faith of the people. It is more to the point to ask whether either man had any notion whatever of a civil religion. This certainly would not preclude a later generation seeing it there, but I am confident that had Jefferson become convinced that he was promoting a civil religion, he would have been unwilling to continue that course. Only if one equates freedom or liberty as principles with religion would one be able to make any other claim for the early inhabitants of the White House.

For Jefferson, and for his true disciples, the influences that motivated action were fruitages of the eighteenth-century European scene and the Enlightenment. If one were to create a civil religion from the ideas of these founding fathers, it would be comparable to the official establishment of Deism. While this might seem superior to some of the recent alternatives promoted in the White House, it would be no less a violation of the Bill of Rights. And Deism reduced to creed would prove just as obnoxious to a free people.

Type B. The other approach which developed from colonial days is characterized by a Calvinist orthodoxy which assumed that religion and politics were in tension until the latter was tamed by the former. Accepting the Puritan aims, Type B sought to ward off potential evil with the whole armor of God. Righteousness was a goal for the nation if it understood its true destiny. Applied to its extreme, this became high chauvinism such as that expressed by President McKinley in 1899 when he made the decision to take the Philippines. "There was nothing left for us to do but to take them all, and to educate the Filipinos, and uplift and civilize and Christianize them, and by God's grace do the very best we could by them as our fellowmen for whom Christ also died. . . . put the Philippines on the map of the United States."[5]

Calvinism in America became a theory of national destiny, a "holy experiment" with the nation under God. Ancient Israel became an archetype even as it had been for the early Puritans. As the Hebrews were judged by Yahweh according to their faithfulness, so orthodoxy came to equate national policy with divine design. National success was dependent upon a national righteousness. This moralistic presentiment could mobilize the populace to worthy action, but it often found difficulty in shaking loose from the intolerance toward other dissent—a mark of its heritage. Calvinism sought to implement a king's chapel in a king's court without the religious establishment.

The history of Calvinism is the story of the major Protestant thrust in America. It is the term which best describes the "mainstream" of English dissent. Continental ecclesiastical groups of the Reform tradition belong in the same classification. Baptist and Presbyterian, Quaker and Methodist have been absorbed into what becomes less theologically pure the more it extends its inclusiveness. Not all persons who bear one of these religious labels necessarily fit into the aforementioned pattern. However, the traditions which carry these names are inclined to support an American "Messianism." This amalgam grew rapidly following the Great Awakening, and in the twentieth century it has supplied Presidents of strikingly different character—Wilson and Nixon, Truman and Eisenhower. Each of these men had a common element of religious heritage which at points was stronger than political moorings.

Type C. Finally, we direct attention to Anglicanism, the "via media" of Henry VIII and Elizabeth. English history supplies ample reason to view this tradition as the middle way, the "centrist" religious option plotting its course between the Puritans and the Catholics in sixteenth- and seventeenth-century Britain. From Hooker to Newman to Maurice to Temple, an atmosphere of unique proportions prevailed. In America, in spite of revolutionary reverses, Episcopalianism survived and blossomed. For many it became synonymous with a Protestant Establishment. It was not the religion on the make; it had already made it. It alone had the variegated background that offered doctrinal breadth and fluidity. Episcopalianism viewed politics and religion in perfect harmony, each with its own sphere. Bound by neither narrow orthodoxy nor unbending principles, it produced a kind of realistic pragmatism. Far more than Type A, the Episcopalian takes the institutions of religion seriously, positively. Freed of utopianism and ideological snags, the third way is one that allows for freedom in movement from church to state and back again. It is not self-conscious about its faith. Post-Vatican II liberal Catholics appear to have found their place in Type C. Although some would say it was Kennedy's "patrician" background that caused the affinity with Roosevelt more than any religious considerations, the religious connections are too striking to ignore.

The three types delineated above allow for at least one generalization. In the present ethical discourse among theologians Type A would best be described as "goal oriented" in approach. Type B fits the ethicist's category of legalism, a grounding in the past laws and doctrines. Thus Type C is properly defined as "situation ethics." This is not meant to be an airtight scheme. There are obvious ambiguities, and no human being can be cast according to a predescribed formula without distorting the man. With this reservation firmly established there follows here a chart indicating the placement of some, not all, of the Presidents according to the pattern just presented.

Type A	*Type B*	*Type C*
John Adams	Andrew Jackson	George Washington
Thomas Jefferson	U. S. Grant	Franklin Pierce
John Q. Adams	Grover Cleveland	Chester Arthur
Abraham Lincoln	William McKinley	Franklin Roosevelt
Andrew Johnson	Theodore Roosevelt	John F. Kennedy
	Woodrow Wilson	
	Warren Harding	
	Calvin Coolidge	
	Herbert Hoover	
	Harry Truman	
	Dwight Eisenhower	
	Lyndon Johnson	
	Richard Nixon	

It is important to emphasize that the types provided apply only to the presidency. There are many other varieties of religious expression in America, but there have been no Lutheran or Jewish or Pentecostal or Black Presidents. It is also evident that since the Civil War the predominant type has been Calvinist.

As we assess the work of some of the men who have held the nation's highest office, we shall be concerned to depict the various ways in which religion was an important factor in their administrations.

There is nothing particularly startling about the suggestion of nationalized religion in the United States. Ancient Rome had its religious cult to which the early Christians refused adherence. The refusal was predicated upon the conviction that such allegiance was a diminution of God through an unholy dual alliance. To the polytheistic community and its leadership the Christian response was madness. The Roman rulers never appeared to understand the nature of monotheism, and as a consequence the early believers were frequently persecuted. The civil religion, which even then was somewhat amorphous, insisted upon the subordination of monotheism to the good of the state. Modern parallels are not difficult to find.

During the forties, the Second World War era, a similar persecution faced Jehovah's Witnesses when they refused to pledge allegiance to the American flag in public schools. For most Americans the pledge was synonymous with patriotism. The salute to the flag and the national anthem were semi-religious rites in the minds of many in a nation at war. Few understood the "madness" of the Witnesses. When ultimate loyalty to the state was demanded and refused, punitive action inevitably followed. In the first decision on the subject in 1940 the United States Supreme Court found for the public school against the recalcitrant children. A 1943 reversal directed a different light upon the subject of loyalty as well as the Bill of Rights. Mr. Justice Jackson, speaking for the Court, expressed the following, now classic, sentiments.

> Those who begin coercive elimination of dissent soon find themselves exterminating dissenters. Compulsory unification of opinion achieves only the unanimity of the graveyard. . . . If there is any fixed star in our constitutional constellation, it is that no official, high or petty, can prescribe what shall be orthodox in politics, nationalism, religion, or other matters of opinion or force citizens to confess by word or act their faith therein.[6]

Unfortunately, wherever there is institutionalized religion, sectarian or governmental, there arises a creed, a dogma, which rapidly subverts the intention of the original. The threat of this is evident in the book by J. Paul Williams in which he urges that in order to preserve the "values shared by all" the nation must see to it that "government agencies . . . teach the democratic ideal as a religion."[7] Since, he says, democracy is the will of God, it "must become an object of religious dedication."[8] He concludes, "systematic and universal indoctrination is essential in the values on which a society is based, if that society is to have any permanence or stability."[9]

As early as the beginning of the nineteenth century, "the old idea of American Christians as a chosen people who had been called to a special task was turned into the notion of a

chosen nation especially favored."[10] It is more accurate to say
that the seeds of such attitudes about the idea of a chosen nation
lie in the fabric of the chosen people concept itself, not in its
corruption. Even if one goes back to the eighteenth century, it
was not the Christian churches that cherished real liberty; it
was Jefferson, Madison, and Paine. The roots of the Bellah ideal
appear in Jeffersonian enlightenment, not in the religious tradition of the nation.

We have to face the fact that only as churches have suffered persecution have they sought freedom, a freedom which,
once attained, they quickly denied to the "infidel." We are at
best on uncertain ground in claiming for the American
churches the role of champion of religious freedom. It was the
intellectual community of the Enlightenment under enthroned
reason which inspired Jefferson and Madison. Either figure
might find election to office difficult today because of this. And
no civil religion is likely to be in the image of the Enlightenment, for that would be a contradiction. Of course, there is
always the danger of deifying reason, but this hardly seems a
present-day option.

For most citizens the words of Jefferson carry weight because he was a "founding father." It is the awe of discovering, in
a tour of Williamsburg, where he sat during services at Bruton
Parish Church. The modern citizen does not elevate Jefferson to
national "sainthood" on the basis of his thought. Raised to
semi-divine status, the third President may be quoted indiscrimi-
nately to buttress all popular causes. And since it is the people
who have canonized Jefferson, who is Robert Bellah to tell them
what he really meant in his writings? In fact, if the majority of
citizens clearly understood the "Sage of Monticello," they
would likely not have elevated him in the first place.

Is there a civil religion today? I think there is a fluctuating
cultus with a tripartite history. The early Presidents were of
Type A and Type C, with the Jeffersonian influence heavy even
among those of the latter group. The Deist mentality was highly

significant until the election of Andrew Jackson. With him the aristocracy of the intellect was cracked, and popularized religion began to influence political style and candidate choice. The growing emphasis upon denominational loyalty during that time also had its effect upon the national mind. "The institutionalization of the kingdom of Christ was naturally accompanied by its nationalization."[11] In the latter portion of the nineteenth century Type C slowly gave way to the rule of Type B. The interlude of Lincoln and Johnson was the last real thrust of Type A, and after 1868 the presidency more and more moved almost exclusively to the Calvinists. A burgeoning nation and expanding denominations found, by the close of the nineteenth century, the presidency reflecting the view that only Christian politics was good politics.

In what follows we shall trace, beginning with Woodrow Wilson, the role of religion in political decision making. Because the President represents all the people in foreign affairs, his dominance as a personality is far clearer in international matters. Domestic issues fragment to such an extent that often the President is forced to see his decisions in terms of the art of the possible. As we shall show in Chapter VI, there is no paucity of moral issues on the domestic scene, and in some instances the personality of the President is vital; but on internal issues the President is controlled by party tradition far more than in foreign affairs. A thorough investigation of the religious roots of political parties would be most desirable. Professor V. O. Key has made much progress in the area of the sociological foundations of political parties.

Because of this "subordination of ideology to politics"[12] on the domestic scene, a much clearer projection of presidential personality can be obtained through a study of foreign policy. Once established, this may be instructive in assessing the efforts toward economic and social justice within the country. There appears a correlation which avoids the conclusion that on domestic issues one must apply only cynicism as a yardstick.

The only answer to a strategy of victory for the Communist world is a strategy of victory for the free world.
—RICHARD M. NIXON

III • *The Flowering of American Messianism*

1 • SHATTERED DREAMS

For liberty is a spiritual conception, and when men take up arms to set other men free, there is something sacred and holy in the warfare.
—WOODROW WILSON

Professor Louis Hartz of Harvard University, speaking before the Senate Foreign Relations Committee in 1968, discussed the problem of revolution. He commented on a potential "nationalist Americanism" which he believed broke onto the stage of history in 1917.

> The matter of the nationalist response goes back, in fact, to the moment of the migration itself. For when the English Puritan comes to America, he is no longer completely "English," which means that he has to find a new national identity. And where is that identity to come from if not from Puritanism itself, the ideal part which he has extracted from the English whole and which alone he possesses. Hence the part becomes, as it were, a new whole and Puritanism itself blossoms into "Americanism."[1]

The term Americanism did not appear until the twentieth century when "collectivists have replaced aristocrats as the symbol of alien ideology."[2] Hartz believes that a new type of American "Messianism" began with President Woodrow Wilson and that it was coincident with the rise to power of Nikolai Lenin. Hence, there was "a tug of war between two attitudes . . . one, the Wilsonian attitude of seeking to impose our institutions, seeking to evangelize the results of a peculiar experience, and another which seeks to recognize the relativity of historical situations and to work within that relativity."[3]

Close scrutiny of the addresses and speeches of President Wilson bears out this observation, and it is evident that Wilson saw most political decisions in moralistic terms. In November of 1918 the President expressed himself in this manner:

> God has in His good pleasure given us peace. It has not come as a mere cessation of arms, a mere relief from the strain and tragedy of war. It has come as a great triumph of right. Complete victory has brought us, not peace alone, but the confident promise of a new day as well in which justice shall replace force and jealous intrigue among the nations. Our gallant armies have participated in a triumph which is not marred or stained by any purpose of selfish aggression. In a righteous cause they have won immortal glory and have nobly served their nation in serving mankind. God has indeed been gracious.[4]

This is an indication that the First World War symbolized the development of America's self-conscious international involvement. The war also marked the beginning of the movement of world Communism. The American populace was well prepared for its entry upon the world scene in the guise of deliverer as a result of the self-esteem created for itself under the influence of President Theodore Roosevelt.

In the year 1923, shortly before his death, Woodrow Wilson wrote to his former Secretary of War, Ray Stannard Baker, "I know of no man who has more perverted the thinking of the world than Karl Marx . . ."[5] Historical evidence attests to the fact that devotion to the Communist world mission is matched by an American missionism.

> To be sure the Americans had a sense of mission, but instead of involving a Trotskyite concept of subversion, it involved the notion of a special purity preserved in the New World, of a "little Israel," as Cotton Mather put it. And yet, as it happened, the force of national power brought America onto the world scene at precisely the moment that world communism became grounded in an effective Bolshevik force. The First World War, in fact, can be viewed as the symbol of both developments.[6]

Wilson's career is unparalleled in the annals of the American presidency. He was a scholar, a successful writer, a university professor and president of an Ivy League institution, a state governor, and a totally committed Presbyterian. All this was deposited in the White House in 1913. Thomas Woodrow Wilson was born of Christian parents and reared accordingly. His father was a Presbyterian minister of considerable gifts. During his son's early years the father served congregations in Virginia, Georgia, and North Carolina. Some critics have insisted that Wilson had an abnormal relationship with his father. In a psychological study of the President, Sigmund Freud and William C. Bullitt accuse Wilson of an overdependency on his father, partially because he never made major decisions without consulting him. With typical Freudian lingo Wilson is caricatured beyond recognition. This attempted postmortem psychoanalysis was risky business at best. And as a reading of the volume reveals, the Freudian terminology in the hands of the "master" applied to a person he never knew can be devastatingly simplistic. Further, Mr. Bullitt had become thoroughly disenchanted with Wilson in 1919 through what he considered a rebuff.[7]

We can only conjecture concerning the nature of Wilson's childhood, but by the time he was in his late teens correspondence supplies ample material for understanding the father-son relationship. An objective reading of the letters affirms that the relationship was hardly unhealthy. One easily detects what once the elder Wilson described as friendship born of respect, not dependent on family ties. The two men had common intellectual interests and these they shared. Only a biased observer would interpret consultation with his father as a sign of weakness or sickness. The world itself would be ill-served if every son were required, in order to be mentally healthy, to turn from seeking guidance from his father.

A Southern Calvinist minister, Joseph Wilson reared young Woodrow to appreciate the culture of the South, though he was never wedded to it. There is little question but that the elder Wilson affected his son's religious thought profoundly. Wilson's deep sense of morality coupled with the Calvinistic understanding of the sovereign God undoubtedly came about from hearing the words of his father from the pulpit. In the year 1874 Wilson wrote: "I am in my 17th year and it is sad, when looking over my past life, to see how few of those seventeen years I have spent in the fear of God, and how much time I have spent in the service of the Devil. . . . If God will give me the grace, I will try to serve him from this time on, and will."[8]

This strong sense of moral righteousness was soon coupled with the assumption that America was the handmaiden of the Lord to achieve his purposes on the earth. Wilson came to the White House as the most Christian of Presidents. He had an unswerving faith in the capitalist system of free enterprise, and as chief executive he was responsible for setting the tone of the United States government in international relations just as the Communist-capitalist engagement began. His religion and his politics combined to cause negative response to the Communist revolution in Russia. Crane Brinton recently gave some clues as to why Communist revolutions are so obnoxious to Americans.

I think one obvious one, of course, is Americans more surely than any Western peoples, except possibly the Swiss, have a firm belief, I won't quite say a religious one, but it is a part of our world attitude, in what we call free enterprise. This is something that in this country isn't just an economic doctrine, it is an emotional belief, and, of course, the Russians starting back with Lenin just did away with free enterprise completely. Second, there is, of course, the fact that the Communist revolutions from the start were anti-Christian, and this country, again has in our own time, I think, become increasingly Christian.[9]

Opposition to the Russian Revolution and to succeeding social revolutions has been due to many factors, not the least of which has been the Communist label. However, it is also true that for the most part world revolutions since 1917 have been social revolutions and the United States understands only political revolution. This may well be why so many in the nation accused Martin Luther King, Jr., of Communist leanings. He was involved in a social revolution in this country, and most Americans have little appreciation for such unrest, categorizing all of it as a front for Communist conspiracy. The FBI smear of Dr. King merely enhanced the public misunderstanding of the man. Since the time of Wilson our national stance has been generally reactionary, a reaction that hardly implements the acceptance of Jeffersonian ideals of freedom beyond our borders, but rather seeks to impose Jefferson's conclusion upon the rest of the world. And one must distinguish the principles upon which Jefferson based his conclusions from those conclusions. If we fail to do so, we may be astonished when the free ballot does not appeal to the poverty-ridden as much as free food.

We might profitably digress at this juncture to ask some questions about the American sentiment concerning her great men. The question is whether America rests upon a rational understanding of its history or upon a mythologizing of that history. For example, perhaps the Jefferson Memorial is appropriate. When one finds himself in that lovely monument at the close of the day and the sun silhouettes the bronze statue against a background of cherry blossoms, he is suddenly conscious of the words inscribed around the rotunda, "I have sworn upon the altar of God, eternal hostility against every form of tyranny over the mind of man." In the cool of a spring afternoon the emotional response may be that such sentiment is marvelous because it was spoken by the "high priest" of American democracy. In that case the words may only have a pleasant ring and not convey any meaning at all. On the other hand, one might read the words, ponder them, and find therein an exciting idea and thus justification for honoring the man who spoke the words, for they are rational and true words for a democracy.

The first approach mentioned here, the mythological one, seems the most common and becomes a possible basis for a civil religion. Since a mythological interpretation may be pronounced by the Puritan, the Anglican, the Deist, or whomever, there may be several different responses. If, on the contrary, one employed his reason to interpret words of the ancient heroes, he might separate the good from the poor ideas and find the pearls of great value. He would avoid the dogmatism that so easily accompanies the "deification" of legendary figures whose ideas are either difficult to understand or seemingly impossible to realize. Further, it might help to assess objectively the strengths and weaknesses of the greatest of the founding fathers.

Communism is a scare word, a terror word. It has been so ever since Attorney General A. Mitchell Palmer moved against the "Reds" in 1920 in such violent fashion that he has been compared with Senator Joseph McCarthy.[10] Palmer actually tried to deport *citizens* who were "suspect." President Wilson, burdened by the problem surrounding the League of Nations and a victim of almost complete physical breakdown in 1919, was in no condition to bridle the Palmer excesses. Although

Wilson had cautioned Palmer not to "let the country see red," the nation was treated to horrendous behavior on the part of governmental officials, so much so that some scholars feel there was, after a time, general revulsion against the entire affair. Eventually, what really turned America away from the "red menace" was an isolationism which followed the election of Warren Harding. Perhaps it was the rejection of the League, possibly disillusionment with the recent war, or even a too quick taste of being international, but whatever it was, a reversal in the country gave it "Normalcy" and Harding in 1921.

The seeds of antagonism to Communism rooted in the early days of Wilson. His 1923 remark could have been anticipated from his university days at Princeton and Virginia. While there is little in his correspondence of those days concerning specific religious beliefs, the letters show a high degree of moralizing which was later easily transferred to his conviction about America's role in the world.[11]

Two distinct characteristics emerge in the early Wilson. First, he was a sensitive, moral man. Whether in the crucial question of marriage in 1885 or the struggle with the Princeton community and Dean West over the placement of the graduate college in 1910, firm ethical conviction dominated him. Second, woven into the fiber of his life was a tenacious refusal to accept constructive criticism. As a resident professor at Bryn Mawr College, he was available to serve as a writer of brief comments on the Washington political scene for *Bradstreets* in New York. On one occasion Mr. Bradstreet took it upon himself to offer some friendly advice on Wilson's style. The indignation of the young professor was so extreme that he almost severed a productive relationship. It does not appear that this harsh response to criticism was due to any religious outlook, but was a personality fault. His father often chided him for his pride as a major weakness.

Wilson entered upon the presidency in 1913 with the pat-

DISCUSSING THE LEAGUE TO ENFORCE PEACE

Darling in the New York *Tribune*

terns of his moral life largely determined. He viewed problems through moral spectacles. His policies, while supported by as scholarly an understanding of the American scene as had ever occupied the White House, were nonetheless controlled by religious perceptions and underlying presuppositions about man and God.

From his lofty pinnacle of power the President may exercise considerable moral leadership. Using that power Wilson had led the nation in fighting a war on moral grounds, and he then sought a peace on the same principles. Those who had heard and heeded him on war were deaf to his pleadings for peace. His grand scheme dissolved into the "Roaring Twenties." In one of his last acts as President, Wilson continued to exhibit moral courage as he vetoed the Prohibition enforcement act.

While many leaders tired of his moralizing, his strength and courage have been unsurpassed in the century, and his ethical sensitivity was at once the backbone of much that he achieved and more that he conceived.

Was Wilson the fashioner of a civil religion? In 1896 Wilson spoke to the Princeton University community. "There is nothing that gives such pith to public service as religion. A God of truth is no mean prompter to the enlightened service of mankind; and character formed as if in His eye has always a fibre and sanction such as you shall not obtain for the ordinary man from the mild promptings of philosophy."[12] Again, "Religion, conceive it but liberally enough, is the true salt wherewith to keep both duty and learning sweet against the taint of time and change . . ."[13] At least the President had a strong sense of moral obligation in the office, however he might ritualize it.

The nature of Wilson's piety was never in doubt. It was sectarian orthodox Calvinism, but it was not nearly so narrow as some have depicted. "I believe," Wilson wrote, "that too much effort is made to get people to believe for fear of the consequences of unbelief. I don't believe any man was ever drawn into heaven for fear he would go to hell. Because, if I understand the Scriptures in the least, they speak of a gospel of love. Except God draw you, you are not drawn."[14] There is predestination without the harshness. What Wilson was expressing was Puritan moralism grounded in a strong theological base. He affirmed the proposition of divine involvement and judgment in history. A biographer, Arthur Link, notes this, and it is quite evident in Wilson's speeches.[15] Wilson believed in the dynamic providence of God; that is, he was assured that there was moral direction in the universe, but he was unwilling to document the future in the light of that plan. His assurance came from the New Testament, particularly the moral admonitions of Jesus. The Bible was the key. His total confidence on this matter is clear in the following sentence. "A man has found himself when he has found his relation to the rest of the universe, and here is the book [Bible] in which these relations are set forth."[16]

The President worked diligently during the post-war era to rehabilitate the devastated Russian people and provide for financial assistance. To that end he enlisted the aid of John Foster Dulles. However, the idealism of a young admirer of those days, William C. Bullitt, was shattered by Wilson's failure to listen to his program for bringing Russia into the community of nations. Wilson's refusal to hear his plan while he was in Paris may explain the derogatory image of the President that we have already noted in the book which Bullitt coauthored with Freud. The Communist issue was already, for Wilson, an ideological engagement, though not yet focused totally within the Soviet Union. Wilson did feel a warmth of affection for people in the mass and for inhabitants of all nations, friend and foe. In his war message to Congress he noted respect and concern for the German people. But his Puritan moralism that motivated that concern also generated a rising American "Messianism." Wilson was no fanatic like Palmer, whose Quaker heritage was hardly evident in his 1920 "red purge." But who can say to what extent the ethical rigidity of the President encouraged the extremities of a Palmer or, later, of a Joe McCarthy?

Critical appraisal of Woodrow Wilson must depend upon proper regard for the Puritanism which inspired the League of Nations. It may be too much to expect one man to impregnate the world with a plan, no matter how imperfect, to unite the planet in peace and to bring that dream to fruition as well. Had Wilson succeeded the world would have been different, but no one can be quite sure in what fashion. Tragically, his vision was obliterated by a nation that was not hearing him, had not been hearing him since 1916, that gave him the presidency by the narrowest of margins in that year and provided him with a succession of Republican Congresses. Even the League plan was flawed with Wilson's too simple messianic understanding of the United States.

Wilson's religious efforts for freedom and peace were posited upon a disappearing Protestant aristocracy and an assumption of favored status for America before the Almighty. To the extent that his aims may become our aims they must find new rationale for the future. Richard Nixon cannot be a successful Wilson in 1972 by emulating him. It is not required of the historian to condemn Wilson's vision either because of its moralistic source or because of the obvious blind spots in Wilson himself. An idea may have birth from a variety of opinions, some mutually exclusive, but the insight is not thereby invalidated. It is our ability to extract those ideas which have value from each era and then to act upon them which demonstrates that we have profited from history. Viewed in this light, Woodrow Wilson is a rich source. In no sense can we resurrect either the man or the conditions of the past. It is ideas, newly formulated and made realistic in implementation, that give promise for this democratic nation.

2 • NORMALCY?

God! What a job.
—WARREN G. HARDING

In 1921 Wilson's "New Freedom" was swallowed up in the Harding "non-presidency." It may be ludicrous even to attempt an analysis of religious influences in a man so unfortunate as Warren Gamaliel Harding. It is regularly contended that Harding was a weak man influenced by evil friends. Standard judgment agrees with Alice Longworth, who said, "Harding was not a bad man, he was just a slob."[17] It is reported that Wilson said of Harding that he was the possessor of a "bungalow mind." No one has yet had the audacity publicly to suggest that Harding might have been a thoroughly corrupt man with weak friends. At least it is worth a thought.

Warren Harding was no aristocrat, no ideologue, no charismatic leader. He merely filled a gap. Had Theodore Roosevelt lived, he well might have been the Republican candidate in 1920. It might also have been General Leonard Wood or possibly Herbert Hoover. That it was Harding finds explanation in the now classic story of the smoke-filled room. The political bosses made him the candidate, and the mood of the nation made him President. Harding was atypical—not that his political philosophy, to the extent that he had one, was markedly different from his two successors. Rather, he seemingly had no sense of either purpose or direction that was unrelated to his personal gratification. He was not even certain the presidency was for him, but was persuaded. His mistresses and his other activities consumed his time and energy far more than those who knew him might have anticipated. In most instances the office of the President has tended to raise mediocre men to a higher level. When asked how this had operated for Harding,

THE CANDIDATE FOR REELECTION

"I'll have to figure out some kind of new slogan."

Alley in the Memphis *Commercial-Appeal*
Used by permission.

one highly respected historian of the period could only recall that Harding was concerned that whiskey bottles not litter the White House. It just wasn't proper. Historians are generally agreed that Harding reversed the process and brought the office to the level of his own mediocrity.

Nominally a Baptist, it is unfair to make any observations on that affiliation. Harding joined the Baptist church in Marion, Ohio, after his political position suggested the wisdom of the move. He may well be his own category where ethics were neither involved nor consciously rejected, but consistent with our earlier projection, he fits in Type B. He was, it seems, as amoral as he was atypical.

Some national progress was recorded in the early twenties, and fair historians have properly credited Harding with a concern for peace. Again, it was Harding who freed Eugene Debs from prison, an act which Wilson refused to grant for the Socialist leader.

Harding's religious affiliation, which made him a "pillar in the local Baptist church," had little evident effect, but his place of birth and the cultural patterns of his youth did convince him of the uniqueness of the United States as God's nation. His three heroes were Caesar, Napoleon, and Alexander Hamilton. Harding was convinced that without Hamilton there would have been no Republic. And of that Republic he said, "God must have destined that the old world should learn of the new . . ."[18]

The most incisive comment on Harding's religion comes from a recent biographer, Francis Russell.

> Religion was for Harding like the Constitution, something to be honored and let alone. As a member of the First Baptist Church, he attended as often as a politician should, listening blankly to the sermon and shaking hands with the pastor on the steps afterward, but the religious preoccupation of his mother and brother and sisters had never touched him. There must be some reason for everything, he believed—in the odd moments when he thought about it—a God somewhere, an afterlife some-

how in which one would not be judged too harshly for brass rails and poker games and the occasional midnight visits to the houses by the railroad station.[19]

Harding's mother had become a fervent Seventh-Day Adventist during his youth, but he was unimpressed with her extreme views and fell easily into the religious tradition of his father. We have to conclude that not every person associated with a church is significantly influenced by that relationship. For many Americans, and Warren Harding seems to have been one of them, church attendance was just the socially acceptable thing.

Harding's death remains clouded in some mystery. There are those who doubt the official explanation and look for possible evidence of suicide. If Harding is to be classified as a tragic figure, it is no less true to say that it was a tragic time for the nation. There is considerable evidence that when Harding died the outpouring of grief was extensive and genuine, but no figure in history more aptly fits Mark Antony's description: "The evil that men do lives after them, the good is oft interred with their bones."

3 • KEEPING COOL

I have never been hurt by what I have not said.
—Calvin Coolidge

The Vice-President under Harding was John Calvin Coolidge, who fitted the times like a glove. His quiet New England manner reassured a restive nation and even the Harding scandals were put aside by the electorate in 1924 as Coolidge won election in his own right. The new President was convinced of the necessity of avoiding any and all government action whenever and wherever possible. For this reason Calvin Coolidge undertook almost no government action programs. Frederick Lewis Allen aptly described the Coolidge era in one sentence. "The great god business was supreme in the land, and Calvin Coolidge was fortunate enough to become almost a demi-god by doing discreet obeisance before the altar."[20] There were no issues except crime and booze. Political discussion nearly departed the land. In the election of 1924 the Communist William Z. Foster polled only 33,000 votes. The Communist issue, like other issues, remained dormant throughout the administration. Samuel Eliot Morison viewed the low Communist vote as a tribute to the average American's faith in his country and its institutions. One wonders why it is a tribute to Americans that they were most complacent and satisfied when there were no issues raised and there was no progress toward justice.

John Calvin Coolidge had a "formless" church background, though he attended the Edwards Congregational Church in Northampton, Massachusetts. He had an amorphous concept of God, well expressed in a speech he made while president of the Massachusetts legislature in 1914, when he said: "Inspiration has always come from above."[21] He was a good-hearted man who believed in the wealth of the nation and its business enterprises. He did not join a church in Washington during his Vice-Presidency, but upon assuming office as President he united with the First Congregational Church in the Capital: "Without fuss or publicity, he joined a church for the first time in his life."[22] This affiliation was a permanent one, for even after he left the White House he and his wife attended regularly. William Allen White wrote of Coolidge that he was "all his life deeply religious." He attended Sunday School and was taught to "work and to save."[23] White records that he was a Calvinist, a Puritan who believed in the sanctity of private property. If the theological underpinnings were far less ideologically restrictive than they had been for Wilson, business had been enthroned in that New England community on the Horatio Alger model.

In his autobiography,[24] Coolidge gives some attention to his faith, enough to suggest that he viewed himself as an instrument in the hands of Deity. He saw himself as open to respond to events. And he does not appear to have been a predestinarian. His failure to affiliate with a church was partially due to a feeling that he might not set a proper example. His decision to join in 1923 was only made after the minister observed him taking Communion and had the congregation vote Coolidge into membership.

A biographer, Donald McCoy, speaks rather movingly of the Coolidge faith.

> Although his ideas of God and religion were mystically vague, it was clear he believed that man had a duty under God's laws to give service. Yet there was no reason why service could not be both pleasant and profitable. . . . He believed in man's perfectibility, in terms of honesty, dependability, industry, service, fairness, kindliness, tolerance, and harmoniousness. The problem was that he did not know how wide the gap was between belief and achievement.[25]

Other perspectives of Coolidge supply a plethora of options, depending upon what one wishes to see in the man. One observer of the twenties spoke of Coolidge as "a seventeenth century orthodox Christian with simple unbending faith."[26] Herbert Hoover gave the most unlikely portrait when he wrote that Coolidge "was a fundamentalist in religion, in the economic and social order, and in fishing."[27] Arthur Schlesinger saw his religion as merely business. Probably what characterized the man best was the phrase "moral power." In his own assessment, Coolidge averred: "The success which is made in any walk of life is measured almost exactly by the amount of hard work that is put into it. . . . The nation with the greatest moral power will win."[28]

Calvin Coolidge had a common understanding of the Christian faith as it was preached in New England. His rearing had been mildly Calvinist, but with a touch of that Unitarian influence that could cause him to speak of the perfectibility of man. He translated his faith into thrift and hard work. He never had a thought that government should actively promote justice and equity. If a man had moral power he would succeed in business and the business of government is business.

The most remarkable thing about the Coolidge years was not the religion of the President but the national cult of the big-business god. The almost unbelievable emphasis on success in material goods and its alliance with "good" religion dominated the national scene. The Social Gospel born out of New York's Hell's Kitchen was buried under the new "greenback gospel." The church went "bananas" along with the rest of the institutions of the time.

The most amazing "religious" publication associated with the twenties was a book by Bruce Barton entitled *The Man Nobody Knows.*[29] Jesus was depicted as the "Man" who really was a topflight salesman and talented executive, molding twelve men into an all-time best management team. Jesus was "the most popular dinner guest in Jerusalem," and an "outdoor man." In fact, Jesus founded modern business. As a satirical "Penultimate" column in the *Christian Century* one might find this language highly amusing, but as the best-selling nonfiction work in America for the years 1925 and 1926, it only makes one wish he hadn't heard about it. Barton made Russell Conwell, "foremost clerical exponent of Andrew Carnegie's 'Gospel of Wealth,' "[30] seem somehow clean by comparison. Make no mistake, the Coolidge years had their roots in Carnegie and Conwell. As the latter once opined: "In this life a man gets about what he is worth, and the world owes a man nothing that he does not earn."[31] In the twenties the return of Herbert Spencer with social Darwinism made the nineteenth century pale in comparison.

In foreign relations Coolidge was somewhat more flexible than Harding had been, but he failed to take the nation into the World Court and left the League altogether to one side. Regarding Russia, the problem was one of diplomatic recognition. Though tempted to consider it, Coolidge backed away. His modified New England orthodoxy avoided the ideological block for Coolidge, but the forces of business would not likely countenance the recognition of a "Collectivist" state. Whereas the clarion cry against Communism in the fifties centered upon its godlessness, in the twenties the issue was economic. Here the twenties probably demonstrated a greater degree of honesty. The failure to recognize the Soviet Union further isolated Russia from the world community. The world will never know what a more progressive policy might have accomplished.

4 • ECONOMIC CHAOS

> The only economic system which will not destroy intellectual and spiritual freedom is private enterprise, regulated to prevent special privilege, or coercion.
> —HERBERT HOOVER

Some historians are convinced that Calvin Coolidge had enough insight into the economy to foresee 1929 and for that reason chose not to run. Others say he did not mean to be taken seriously by the party, that he did want another term. That he withdrew, for whatever reason, provided opportunity to Herbert Hoover, a man who had been seeking the position since 1920. Of the three men who represented the Republican Party in the White House from 1921 to 1933, Hoover was by all odds the most able. He was a person of broad international experience and business know-how, a prosperous engineer, and

"HERBERT!"

Cargill in the Jersey *Journal*

a self-made man. A graduate of the Harvard of the West, he was
justifiably proud of his association with Stanford University as
a member of its first graduating class. Leland Stanford seemed
to epitomize the Hoover doctrine of success.

Herbert Hoover was reared a Quaker and adhered to that
sect throughout his life. In his *Memoirs* he described the early
days in the Quaker meeting with its strict rules of discipline and
its biblical fundamentalism. Yet in all his discussion of that
early period of his life, he does not indicate the personal effect,
if any, that the faith had upon him. Later generations, however,
have tended to attribute to his religious heritage his well-earned
title of "Humanitarian." Certainly his efforts on behalf of starving refugees was consistent with Quaker virtues.

By 1910 Herbert Clark Hoover had amassed a personal
fortune as an engineer, and during the days prior to the War
he was spending the majority of his time working for the development of various business interests abroad. During most of
this period he was in England, where he was residing when
hostilities broke out in 1914. His organizational talent was early
employed in relief work on the Continent, especially in Belgium. When he returned to America in 1919 he was something
of a national figure, and Franklin Roosevelt appears to have
urged his election as President. At the time Hoover had not
declared his party connection.

During his European experience Hoover had become disil-
lusioned alike with rampant individualism and socialism. He
returned to the United States speaking of the moral purpose of
America to serve human need through what he described as
"cooperation." This voluntary association for the purpose of
meeting human distress bore the label "progressive individualism." Another word continually appeared in his speeches. It
was the word "compassion." In the election oratory of 1936
Hoover expressed this thought: "We must fight again for a
government founded upon ordered individual liberty and opportunity that was the American vision."[32] He has been

wrongly caricatured as having supported "rugged individual-ism" in its raw sense. This is unfair. The role of government was never to control, but it was to facilitate cooperation. It was this view, based upon a particular philosophy of government, that would finally tie Hoover's hands in the Depression as surely as principle had bound Wilson only ten years before.

Hoover was "self-made," and out of his a٬ ،dance he recognized a moral responsibility to the people. "For Hoover represented, in the highest and best sense, all the virtues of the last Anglo-Saxon-Protestant generation to dominate the American political establishment."[33] A dedicated Calvinist in theology, he was assured that economic success was the result of divine election and virtue.

Hoover's enlightened laissez-faire philosophy—govern-ment could serve by helping people to help themselves—was too little for the Crash of 1929. Hoover was in no way insensi-tive to the needs of the millions affected adversely by the Depression, but according to his political creed there was noth-ing government could do. The fact that the Reconstruction Finance Corporation (RFC) was chartered to salvage busi-nesses was consistent with his principles, since the RFC would aid those businesses to survive and maintain the economy by means of loans. Nevertheless, this apparent favoritism to the corporations inspired a bitterness in the common man that isolated Hoover and made him lonely and bitter by 1933.

In the political debates of 1932 Hoover fought vigorously against the Roosevelt "New Deal." He warned that disaster would overtake the nation if the Roosevelt program were effected. It would destroy individual freedom and liberty. He called it "Collectivism" and defined it as "any system where the tendency is to make the people the servants of the government or personal power as opposed to the government being the servant of the people. That is a complicated idea but it is the age-long fight of human liberty."[34] In spite of his valiant efforts, Hoover was literally smothered in the November election. Historians continue to debate whether Hoover was a victim of circumstances or whether as a part of Republican administrations since 1921 he was one of the architects of the Depression. Hoover himself came to believe that the cause of the debacle lay in foreign influence in the economic sphere, and thus he rejected the internal explanation offered by the Democrats.

The emphasis upon the issue of collectivism was obvious in the campaign of 1928. Mr. Hoover delivered a speech in October of that year warning of the dangers to the American system of government by involvement in business. The seeds were present for later tragic developments.

In the early years in Washington Hoover was a committed internationalist, believing in the League of Nations and the World Court, though he did not press the issue with either Harding or Coolidge. But he had one abiding fear, the fear of Communism. Hoover had always insisted that individualism had to be tempered by "an equality of opportunity."[35] For him American individualism meant that each person would have the opportunity to develop, and this was in contrast to individualism run riot. He did not allow for the fact that equal opportunity is not a once-and-for-all proposition. He did not see society as constantly in the process of creating inequity which required adjustment. He did not have sufficient suspicion of unrestrained individual effort. But no such caution affected him on the left. The real threat to freedom was Communism, and he envisioned the New Deal collectivism as headed toward Communism. By 1938 Hoover had identified Socialism with "its bloody brother communism."[36]

One of Mr. Hoover's earliest tools in the anti-Communist crusade was food. In 1919 Hoover proposed to President Wilson a relief commission for Russia similar to the one for Belgium. He believed that hunger in the Soviet Union could be employed to force the government either to accept the Western desires or to allow the people to starve. The irony was that "the Soviet regime itself was probably saved by Herbert Hoover."[37]

George Kennan has written some penetrating words on this diplomacy.

> The idea of using food as a weapon was one which had a very strong appeal to the American mind. It appealed to some of the most dangerous weaknesses in the American view of international affairs, and had, in my opinion, a most pernicious influence on American thinking. Since the money and the food would be donated by Americans, the action could always be portrayed to the people at home as an altruistic and benevolent one, and made to contrast favorably with that evil and awful thing called "power politics" of which the European countries were presumed to be chronically guilty. No use of force was involved. . . . One simply defined one's conditions and left it to the other fellow to take it or leave it. If he accepted, all right; if he declined, so much the worse for him.[38]

What effect his feelings toward the Soviet Union may have had on the adjustment of reparations for Germany in 1929 we cannot assess. Clearly, Germany was an important buffer against the Soviets.

One major international problem which had far-reaching implications was the Japanese invasion of Manchuria in 1931. This action disturbed the Soviet Union, which sought security through diplomatic relations with the United States. This, however, came to fruition only under the administration of Franklin Roosevelt. When Japan acted in violation of the League of Nations pact, Secretary of State Stimson urged economic sanctions against that nation. China supported this strategy. President Hoover rejected the idea, seeing it as tantamount to a declaration of war. He later contended that the use of such sanctions in 1941 against Japan by the Roosevelt administration helped precipitate the outbreak of war. Many historians conclude that the Second World War began on September 16, 1931. Mr. Hoover did not move to check the aggression. Whatever the reasons, Hoover refused to endorse his Secretary of State on the question of sanctions. It is at least possible to conjecture that President Hoover was not totally displeased with Japanese presence in Manchuria as a buffer against Russian designs in the Far East.

Throughout the administration of the Republicans there was a refusal to recognize the government of Russia. Looking back, Mr. Hoover wrote, "But the denial of recognition kept their potency [for government overthrow] from being serious."[39] In 1933 the United States, now under Democratic control, recognized the Soviet Union. Hoover saw this recognition as the cause of the ensuing problems with the Soviets. It is difficult to determine how much of the venom poured out by Mr. Hoover from 1949 until his death was bitterness generated by being what he considered the victim of bad fortune. Obviously no man desires to have his entire career judged by disaster, and for the most part that is what the American people had done. Perhaps in his effort to regain his lost esteem Mr. Hoover became vituperative. In any event, by 1950 the former President was expressing his ideology in stark terms.

> What the world needs today is a definite, spiritual mobilization of the nations who believe in God against this tide of Red agnosticism. It needs a moral mobilization against the hideous ideas of the police state and human slavery. The world needs mobilization against this creeping Red imperialism. The United States needs to know who are with us in the cold war against these practices, and whom we can depend on.[40]

Moving from this point, Hoover proposed the abandonment of the United Nations in favor of a "cooperation of God-fearing free nations." He concluded, "And in rejecting an atheistic other world, I am confident that the Almighty God will be with us."[41]

Now few would quarrel with Mr. Hoover's revulsion at the totalitarian regime that had grown powerful in the Soviet Union since 1917. Any police state is abhorrent to a free people. The issue is not the rejection of the Communist ideology or the concern over bloody oppression. The issue in America was and is how best this nation can implement its understanding of human freedom.

> The struggle for the minds of men, then, is a task of infinite subtlety and complexity. Nothing is easier, more certain of popular support, and also more certain of failure than to approach so intricate a task in the spirit and with the techniques of a Fourth of July oration.[42]

Herbert Hoover saw red and was afraid. It annihilated a perspective that had favored the League of Nations in 1919. This fear grew in him as the years progressed and reached its zenith just as Senator Joseph McCarthy made his public debut. Hoover had always been a strong supporter of American "Messianism" in foreign policy. He transferred this into a too easy identification of all dissent as Communist or "fellow traveler." In the production of his *Memoirs* Hoover fell before that illogic. He saw Communists as virtually dwelling in the New Deal and recognized little distinction between left-wing and red. He regularly compared Roosevelt to Hitler, Lenin, and Mussolini. He felt the New Deal had subverted the nation.[43]

Hoover's critics have often associated him with the Horatio Alger stories and the image of the self-made man. In June of 1949 Mr. Hoover accommodated his critics. He said he felt comfortable with Alger and Christian in *Pilgrim's Progress*.[44] As his years extended, the former President more and more invoked the Bible and the Christian faith. He spoke often of the Sermon on the Mount as the antidote to Marx. The underlying dynamic of his presidency was probably well represented in these later addresses, expunged of the bitterness. But if one wishes to grasp his utterly simplistic approach to religion it is nowhere better expressed than in the following quotation: "The ethics of good sportsmanship are second only to religious ethics."[45] There in capsule was the tragedy of Herbert Hoover, viewing Christian ethics as little more than good manners. And he was a most mannerly man.

> For those who would keep any group in our nation in
> bondage I have no sympathy or tolerance.
>
> —LYNDON JOHNSON

IV • *From New Deal to Prayer Deal*

1 • PRAGMATISM

> The fight for social justice and economic Democracy
> . . . is a long, weary, uphill struggle.
>
> —FRANKLIN ROOSEVELT

One could hardly say that Franklin Delano Roosevelt made his debut upon the political scene in 1932. Born of patrician parentage in the opulent period of the nineteenth century, he was first involved in politics as early as 1910. He was unexpectedly elected to the New York Senate in that year and served with such distinction that he became known as a major political reformer. As a Democrat he was enchanted with the career of Woodrow Wilson and deeply involved himself in the successful effort to obtain the presidential nomination for Wilson in 1912. When the election was determined, Wilson's Secretary of the Navy brought Roosevelt to Washington as his assistant, and there he remained for the entire Wilson administration. In his new position Roosevelt often experienced frustration with the semi-pacifism of his superior, Josephus Daniels, and another member of the Cabinet, Secretary of State William Jennings Bryan. Roosevelt was convinced that involvement in the European war on the side of the British was inevitable and necessary. In some ways this was a "dry run" for his experience in the thirties with the American public and the pacifist-isolationist bloc. In 1920 he accepted nomination in a hopeless race for Vice-President on the ill-fated Cox ticket. As a referendum on the League of Nations, the election supplied ample notice that America had turned her face from Europe and preferred "Normalcy" to world leadership.

The fateful year of 1921 nearly destroyed the political career of Roosevelt as he suffered a severe attack of crippling polio. Sustained by an indomitable wife, he refused to succumb to his mother's urging to retire, but fought his way back to health in time to nominate his friend Al Smith for President at the 1924 Democratic Convention. Historians note a dramatic change after the illness. Samuel Rosenman, chief speech writer and confidant of the President, discussed the maturity of the man in these words: "This was a new kind of man in politics for me: one who did not seem to care—or even know—whether you were a Catholic, Protestant or Jew."[1]

Governor Smith did not receive the nomination in 1924, but FDR was back at the Convention in 1928 to try again. For a variety of reasons, not the least of which was his stand on prohibition, Smith was defeated by Hoover in the fall election. During that campaign Hoover reiterated his opposition to alcohol and his support of the prohibition amendment. Also, for the first time, the religious issue was injected because Smith was a Catholic.

By 1932 the mood of the country had markedly shifted on the alcohol question, and even the Republicans abandoned the dry stand. Smith had gone down to defeat in 1928, but FDR was elected Governor of New York even in that Republican year. Reelection in 1930 presaged his final arrival on the nascene as the Democratic candidate for President in 1932. During the campaign Walter Lippmann expressed reservation about the Governor, but at no time more pointedly than in February when he wrote: "The judgment exists, and has grown more firm, that he has not got the grasp of the issues or the disinterestedness or the resolution that a President must have in time of great emergency."[2] The 1932 Democratic platform was a return to the Wilson New Freedom more than it was a genuine reflection of what was then called collectivism. Lippmann was more perceptive when he caught the collectivism of Roosevelt "in certain of his moods." But no one seems to have anticipated that the progressivism of Woodrow Wilson would come to fruition in the fertile mind of FDR and his "Brain Trust."

By most accounts Franklin Roosevelt was a religious man. Reared in the aristocratic atmosphere of the Episcopal Church, he remained for his entire life a concerned layman in what he told Harold Ickes was the "low church" tradition. His correspondence makes clear that he found genuine worth in the religious experience. He was not unaware of the political benefits to be garnered from proper use of one's religion, but there is every indication of a sincerity in his private faith equal to that of Wilson. Religion gave Roosevelt a sense of destiny not bound to legalistic determinism but a destiny to be worked out in freedom. He was not susceptible to a strict conscience on public affairs, for he saw morality as ends, not means. "For when the moral cosmology of New Dealism sank beneath the surface, what appeared, of course, was that happy pragmatism which usually refused to concern itself with moral issues at all."[3]

Unless a man carried religion to the extent of President Wilson, it is difficult to unearth the depth of his religious sentiment from speeches and letters. But one of the most cogent expressions of the pragmatic application of FDR's faith came in a 1936 address on the fiftieth anniversary of the Statue of

Liberty. Roosevelt said: "The realization that we are all bound together by hope of a common future rather than by reverence for a common past, has helped us to build upon this continent a unity . . ."[4] Here were freedom and destiny joined.

Intimate friends may tend to gloss the reality, but their testimony is still the next best source of understanding and empathy. One of FDR's closest advisers and the source of a large number of his speeches was Judge Samuel Rosenman. In order for Rosenman to properly capture what Roosevelt wanted to say and translate it into written form, he had to know the man extremely well. Judge Rosenman has left us this portrait.

> While the President was not a regular churchgoer, I always thought of him as a deeply religious man. That he should turn to prayer instead of oratory on the most important day of the war [D-Day] since Pearl Harbor was not surprising; Roosevelt felt a veneration for his Creator which expressed itself often. It was this feeling that made him ask for special church services on particular occasions, such as inauguration days. He was deeply moved during those services, and you could see the effect of them on his face as he left the church to go to the Capitol to take his oath of office. His references to God, so frequent in his speeches, came naturally to him; they were prompted by the same feeling. I have often thought that his deep concern for his fellowmen—even those whom social and financial tradition might call the meanest and the lowliest—had its roots in his religious conviction of the innate dignity of every human being.[5]

Woodrow Wilson had been capable of theologizing like an expert, for he was conversant with the intricacies of biblical scholarship. His religious orientation was essentially Reformed Protestant with its tendency toward ideological expression in doctrine and dogma. This does not imply that Wilson demonstrated religious prejudice in office. Indeed, it was he who appointed Justice Brandeis to the Supreme Court over considerable anti-Semitic sentiment in the nation. But Wilson was restricted by ideology. It was not so with Roosevelt. His religion was a sentiment with no creedal definitions. Though an Episcopalian, he espoused an a-Protestant, a-ecclesiastical position. This was a personal matter with him, not something to be demonstrated at a prayer breakfast or through religious friends and associates. The Bible he saw in essentially ethical terms, and the manifestation of his biblical insights was often militant, possibly as a result of the profound influence of the headmaster of Groton, Endicott Peabody.[6]

The idea of the God to whom he gave allegiance appears in a letter which he wrote to Pope Pius XII in 1939 concerning the faith of the masses.

> They know that unless there is belief in some guiding principle and some trust in a divine plan, nations are without light, and peoples perish. They know that the civilization handed down to us by our fathers was built by men and women who knew in their hearts that all were brothers because they were children of God. They believe that by His will enmities can be healed; that in His mercy the weak can find deliverance, and the strong can find grace in helping the weak.[7]

The point here was not a God who endorsed nationalism but a faith that would bind up the planet's wounds. It is the call to universal faith for the world, rather than the cry for a national cultus which will galvanize the nation for a titanic struggle with the forces of evil. Consciously or otherwise, FDR was here consistent with the thoughts of the great radio preacher of the thirties, Harry Emerson Fosdick, who espoused the "fatherhood of God and the brotherhood of man." Though this was generally criticized by neoorthodox theologians as too simplistic, the effect in inspiring men of goodwill to act for the benefit of humanity causes one to have some serious reservations about the criticism.

Orthodox Christians preferred clear statement of the uniqueness of the faith. In enlightened form they had this in Wilson. Coolidge and Hoover also fit the standard pattern, though the *Christian Century* seemed to have misgivings about whether Hoover would be fit when he took the office. But in Roosevelt the orthodox definitely could not rest easy. He had the same kinds of moral concerns which stimulated his predecessors, but with the distinct difference that his religion had no exclusionist overtones and therefore could not contribute to American "Messianism" or Christian nationalism. This disturbed many of FDR's critics. For him religion was related to culture, and therefore pragmatic solutions to real international problems took account of this fact about ourselves as well as our adversary. Roosevelt might have the same goals but the practical behavior was radically different. The art of compromise was built into the fiber of Roosevelt's faith, a fact that prompted the *Christian Century* in the late forties to describe him as Machiavellian. History has dealt with him more kindly.

It was his relativism that made it possible for Roosevelt to view the Communist question rationally. In the first place, he never accepted the idea that Communism was an international monolith. Indeed, he has been severely criticized for the Yalta Conference of 1945 on just that score. More likely what Yalta reflects is a dying man making unwise decisions. It is not clear that an ideologue at Yalta would have done better. We have no way of ascertaining that.

In 1941 FDR commented upon the Communist question in a revealing way. Again writing to the Pope he said:

> There are in the United States many people in *all* churches who have the feeling that Russia is governed completely by a communistic form of society. In my opinion, the fact is that Russia is governed by a dictatorship, as rigid in its manner of being as is the dictatorship in Germany. I believe, however, that this Russian dictatorship is less dangerous to the safety of other nations than is the German form of dictatorship.[8]

He was correct for 1941 and his opinion stands the test of critical analysis even today. Imagine the Nazi Party in possession of modern weaponry.

The explanation of Roosevelt's reluctance to see Commu-

THE BIG THREE

Courtesy of the Richmond *Times-Dispatch*

nism as a demonic force lies in his refusal to become ideologically bound. His religion was highly personalized but it did not contain the Calvinistic strain so common in mainline Protestantism. Roosevelt was able to avoid the rigid legalism of a moral code which interpreted political issues in terms of ideology. FDR's universalism respecting God made his task far more complex, lacking as he did the neat black and white distinctions about right and wrong.

Roosevelt's pragmatism caused Reinhold Niebuhr to find considerable weakness in the New Deal, and it was not until the election of 1940 that he voted for Roosevelt. Actually, FDR faced considerable opposition from churchmen because he lacked, as they saw it, morality or a sense of mission against worldly evil. Discussing that problem and that particular mentality, Dietrich Bonhoeffer had the following interesting comment. "One of the characteristic features of church life in the Anglo-Saxon countries . . . is the organized struggle of the Church against some particular worldly evil, the 'campaign,' or, taking up again the crusading idea of the Middle ages, the 'crusade.' "[9] This caused the German theologian to question the wisdom of the Church attempting to solve worldly problems.

On the Russian scene, FDR may have blundered badly in his estimation of Stalin as a man. Eleanor Roosevelt commenting on this said, "I think he still thought, however, that in the end he could make Stalin live up to his word, and that he, Stalin, and Churchill, having fought the war together, had gained enough understanding and respect for each other to be able to work things out."[10] Personal diplomacy had its pitfalls, but so has every international policy in a nuclear age.

What was characteristic in diplomacy was apparent in religious thought. Mrs. Roosevelt quoted her husband on the subject after his death.

> I think it is unwise to say you do not believe in anything when you can't prove that it is either true or untrue. There is so much in the world which is always new in the way of discoveries that

it is wiser to say that there may be spiritual things we are simply unable to fathom. Therefore I am interested and have respect for whatever people believe, even if I can not understand their beliefs or share their experiences.[11]

This liberal agnosticism is in marked contrast with the religious view of Dwight Eisenhower, who felt everyone should have some type of belief, no matter what it was. In Roosevelt's case the emphasis fell upon the believing subject, for Eisenhower it was upon the value of the object, the belief itself.

In his application of a religious perspective Roosevelt was often described as cynical. Further, he was accused by some critics of leaning toward Socialism or actually of being a Socialist. This led some right-wing observers to go a step further and accuse FDR of being a Communist. In his *Memoirs* Herbert Hoover all but did exactly that. This identification of FDR as Communist would have been ridiculed on the European continent, where he might well have been categorized as in the same conservative mold as Winston Churchill. The explanation for the unique American attitude comes from the nature of the nation itself. De Tocqueville wrote that Americans were "born equal." This acute insight stems from the historical fact that America never had the feudalism of Europe against which Whigs reacted. There never was the development of the "left" in the United States as a reaction, since feudalism was nonexistent. To be sure, we developed various forms of servitude— slavery, segregation, laissez-faire capitalism—but these were not organic parts of the national tradition and all were antithetical to the Constitution as amended. Consequently, the "left" was frustrated in America, and in this century Marxism has never been a challenge to our system of government. A further safety valve was the American labor movement. Roosevelt recognized this, and it was natural that his critics, having no real "left" to attack, pinned the label on him.

According to Louis Hartz, it was the "American liberal faith" that prevented any success of Marxism.

In other words, the crucial thing was that, lacking the socialist challenge and of course the old corporate challenge on the right such as the European conservatisms still embodied, he [Roosevelt] did not need to spell out any real philosophy at all. His "radicalism" could consist of what he called "bold and persistent experimentation," which of course meant nothing in terms of large social faiths and was indeed perfectly compatible with "Americanism." Good Americans like Edison and Alexander Graham Bell were experimenters. So were the pioneers. When asked concerning his social philosophy, Roosevelt once said that he was a Democrat and a Christian.[12]

Roosevelt produced the New Deal, which his wife called "nothing more than an effort to preserve our economic system."[13] Many, including Judge Rosenman, have claimed that this effort took on the shape of social justice because of FDR's ethical sensitivity. Internationally FDR came to terms with Russia to implement Allied victory in Europe. Many people at that time, and since, suggested that he should have let Russia fail and then this nation could have had the victory to itself. But the modern historian is hard pressed to determine what might have happened in the Second World War without the "Eastern Front." We just do not know. FDR charted a middle course, neither as a starry-eyed idealist nor as a hidebound legalist. He was, as *The New York Times* described the late, great Reinhold Niebuhr, "a political liberal who subscribed to a hard-boiled pragmatism."[14] Roosevelt sought national survival through experimentation. We still have these same tools with which to work that FDR bequeathed us—negotiation and reason.

The death of Franklin Roosevelt was not unexpected by his intimates, as Mrs. Roosevelt noted in her memoirs. Yet, to the nation at large, still unable to see the President on television, the death was a surprising and crushing blow. The new medium of television has created an entirely fresh approach to political events. The assassinations of the sixties suggested a completely new dimension to any prospective civil religion. The propaganda possibilities are staggering if a concerted effort were made to establish a national cult. And of course the horror of war has been enhanced by its proximity in the family room and mitigated when brought with the compliments of a toothpaste company.

Roosevelt was the last President to hold office in the pre-tube era. Since the early fifties, television has played an increasing role in political image building. Daniel Boorstin has drawn a distinction between event in the old era and "pseudo-event" in the present.[15] Religion has its part to play in this image building, and thus analysis of religious commitment becomes far more problematic in the period after 1950. An excellent discussion of the process at work as related to Richard Nixon is to be found in Joe McGinniss' *The Selling of the President 1968*. The 1960 presidential debates were only the first round in the growing role of television in manipulating political events. Only extreme caution by the networks will prevent political parties from such manipulative activity in the future. Mastery of the acting technique can produce instant sincerity by political candidates and the image of the persecuted public official, e.g., Spiro Agnew. Richard Nixon's famous "Checkers" speech of 1952 was the first instance of use of the medium to demonstrate sincerity.

The nation's reaction to FDR's death was similar in many ways to that recorded by the public after the John Kennedy assassination, though here again the intensity of the response in 1963 was conditioned by television. But JFK's death did not strike the nation with any greater force than the announcement in 1945. As many have observed, those who lived through the forties can tell exactly where they were and what they were doing on December 7, 1941, and on April 12, 1945, when the two news stories broke. As a boy of thirteen I was deeply affected, as was my family. To friends and foes alike FDR had *become* the nation. This was achieved because rather than strap an ideology on the country or lead it toward utopian goals, he had succeeded in identifying his actions with America. No doubt he was aided in his image by the Depression and the War, but it seems fair to suggest that Roosevelt neither looked back to an earlier form of a civil religion nor yet promised a humanistic paradise as a substitute for Christianity. FDR became the civil religion in the sense that he represented in his person the character of America. But this never became a cult to any greater extent than people praising the President. There was no ritual of the past or salvation for the future. There was justice and freedom for the present.

The above is not to imply that the nation failed to demonstrate grief at other presidential deaths. There is considerable evidence to the contrary. "What really jolts the situation into perspective, though, is the evidence of rather extravagant displays of grief at the death of President Harding, a man of less heroic stature."[16] Even Harding was bigger than life for the country, but the citizens have not mythologized him in the way they have FDR and JFK. In each case the personal nature of the administration carried over in an appeal to the citizens.

2 • RETURN TO MESSIANISM

> Everyone has the right to express what he thinks. That, of course, lets the crackpots in. But if you cannot tell a crackpot when you see one, then you ought to be taken in.
> —HARRY TRUMAN

If President Roosevelt had tried to select a man of opposite temperament to run with him he could not have done better than with Harry S. Truman. Truman was a self-made Missouri politician. He had served with reasonable distinction in the United States Senate and appeared genuinely reluctant to leave that body to become the Democratic candidate for Vice-President. As one observed the inauguration in January of 1945 it was difficult to imagine a greater contrast than that between the Episcopalian patrician of Groton and Harvard and the Baptist politician from Kansas City. History was to serve Harry Truman better than his dossier.

Unrest reigned in the nation on the brink of military victory, and the restless spirit was unnerving for many months. Evidently Mr. Truman had been privy to no top-level military information, so he went almost "blind" to Potsdam for his meeting with Stalin and Churchill. Only after taking the oath of office was the new President informed of the existence of the atomic bomb.[17]

Immediately upon learning of the bomb, President Truman appointed a committee of knowledgeable men to advise him on its use. The committee consisted, among others, of Dr. Vannevar Bush, Dr. James Conant, and Dr. Karl T. Compton. It was to be advised by a group of scientists which included Dr. J. Robert Oppenheimer. All of these men, along with the rest of the committee, recommended "that the bomb be used against the enemy as soon as it could be done."[18] Before leaving for Potsdam Mr. Truman authorized the use of the atomic bomb if a warning to Japan about the weapon did not produce peace initiative on the part of that government. While in mid-Atlantic returning from Europe the President heard of the bombing of Hiroshima on August 5, 1945. Mr. Truman later commented on the responsibility for the decision to use the deadly new weapon.

> The final decision of where and when to use the atomic bomb was up to me. Let there be no mistake about it. I regarded the bomb as a military weapon and never had any doubt that it should be used. The top military advisers to the President recommended its use, and when I talked to Churchill he unhesitatingly told me that he favored the use of the atomic bomb if it might aid to end the war.[19]

At the time of the explosion there were a few voices raised in protest. The *Christian Century* called it a "moral earthquake." An editorial went on to say, "the churches of America must dissociate themselves and their faith from this inhuman and reckless act of the American government."[20] Significantly, the editor mentioned both Roosevelt and Churchill, but not Truman. It only spoke of "our leaders." The *Century* editor was uttering a prophetic word, but reasonable men would be wise to show caution in assigning moral responsibility for the decision, and more particularly as related to Harry Truman. In retrospect it was a horrendous decision, but one in which the whole nation bore responsibility. The *Christian Century* attacked the bombing as if its own pacifist position of the thirties had contributed nothing to the total world chaos. Its earlier efforts to write a moral ticket for the nation was a constant problem for FDR in dealing realistically with Germany. The *Century* failed to recognize that the churches cannot possibly dissociate themselves from American decisions in foreign policy unless they wish to remain silent on all social and political matters. Prophetic judgment always seems to involve identification with the community, as Isaiah said: "for I am a man of unclean lips and I dwell among a people of unclean lips." The responsibility of the churches to voice a strident protest to unconscionable acts is one born of compassion and "hardboiled realism."

Harry Truman was reared in accordance with the typical pattern of the Midwest and its own peculiar religious heritage. Midwesterners take quite seriously their religion, which is woven into the fabric of the culture as clearly as in any other section of the country. The churches dominated the mores of the community during the nineteenth century in the small towns and even the larger cities. The Trumans lived in Independence, which is now only a few minutes' drive from the center of Kansas City, but was not so in the days of Truman's childhood. The Truman family had moved to Independence when young Harry was six. Mr. Truman says in his *Memoirs* that it was at that time that his parents decided the children should attend Sunday School. They went throughout their childhood to the Presbyterian Church in the neighborhood. Interestingly, Mr. Truman speaks of the church as having served as a kind of social center, but he attributes his "ideals" to his school-teachers and his understanding of the world to an engrossing interest in reading history. He was married in an Episcopal church and his Baptist connection appears to have been formal-ized only in adult life. No matter what direct effect the Sunday School may have had on the boy, the whole community was permeated with the Protestant ethos and consequently with a Calvinistic view of life. Ethics was a personal matter and there was, and still remains in that area, a strong identification of religion with national life. The heartland of America produced Harry Truman in what must be described as a real Mark Twain environment. He liked his childhood, his friends, and his family. Of all the men to occupy the White House since the time of Wilson, he was the most natural, the least self-conscious, the most well-adjusted to his environment.

Harry Truman may not have imbibed the God and coun-try concept from his religious training, but he surely was affected by the Midwest culture in its identification of Chris-tianity as America's religion. All enemies of the faith could be seen as enemies of the nation. Communism was such a menace. In his 1949 inaugural President Truman offered ample evidence both of the ethical dimensions of his personality and his views on Communism. He said that the United States would have no part of the "deceit and mockery" of Communism. He spoke of the "false philosophy" as being over against the moral upright-ness of democracy. It was in that context that he set forth his famous Point Four Program for the relief of world poverty and hunger.[21] With that address the President became the leader of the nation.

Expressing the same idealism that had driven Wilson, Truman closed his inaugural with these words: "Steadfast in our faith in the Almighty, we will advance toward a world where man's freedom is secure. To that end we will devote our strength, our resources, and our firmness of resolve. With God's help the future of mankind will be assured in a world of justice, harmony, and peace."[22] The speech had an almost self-righteous tone calling for a national crusade for freedom grounded in the too neat dichotomy which divides the world in ideological halves of black and white.

Point Four was, of course, in the national interest. In this judgment, however, one needs to be cautious. Those who would fault a Truman or an Eisenhower must at least ask themselves what would "national interest" be without its moral dimension. With all the self-righteousness of our foreign policy, where would the nation be without the Judeo-Christian tradition? Although no certain answer can be supplied, we might profitably observe other nations that struggled to national identity with subsequent denials of freedom. With this in mind, it is certainly unwise for the critic of Puritan ethical dimensions in American policy to be, himself, too self-righteous in his own conceit. A prophetic voice does not require rejection of the essential quality of an enlightened nationalism. And this applies to Vietnam.

There is a tendency, understandable to be sure, to attack hypocrisy in government involvement in Vietnam so as to imply that in the last analysis all morality in government is relative. The argument is that since our government seeks to justify the war on moral grounds and there are no moral grounds for the war, therefore all political morality is suspect. I believe this judgment to be erroneous. To be sure, all morality is related to culture and in that sense no one culture can rightly claim absolute superiority over another. But surely there is a hierarchy of values even within corrupt societies. The very discus-

"NAH! LET'S WAIT TILL THEY GO COMMUNIST,
THEN SPEND A FEW BILLIONS FIGHTING THEM"
From *The Herblock Book* (Beacon Press, 1952)

sion of the topic of ethics and foreign policy is not common-place for all national states. In short, recognition of error does not demand flagellation.

The very fact that American leadership continually seeks to rationalize the Vietnam War on moral grounds says some-thing about the society in which we live even as it points to hypocrisy. There is a public sense that something is amiss in national policy if it lacks moral sanction, and this tradition is not all bad. Certainly it can be bent to perpetuate immoral action with pious support. American "Messianism" often becomes just that. But the Christian ethic has a brighter side in its effect upon the nation. When we charge American leader-ship with hypocrisy, by what norm is it being judged? Is it not the Judeo-Christian morality? The realist who vigorously dis-sents from our policy in Vietnam has a dream for his nation, and his realism will aid in its accomplishment. It should not turn one into a total relativist where beliefs and faiths no longer matter. The obverse of "Messianism" need not be indifference. It might be more intense caring which has a motivation born of respect for the entire human community: a belief that a nation can be better.

It has been argued with some cogency that the Truman "containment" policy of the late forties was the wisest possible action he could have taken. He did begin his administration with a trust for Stalin which rapidly dissipated. The policies of the deceased President Roosevelt could hardly stand against the cold realities of the Soviet Union and the hot rhetoric of Winston Churchill. If there was fault, it lay in Truman's deci-sion to make Communism the issue rather than Russian dicta-torship. Samuel Eliot Morison took the Truman line when he wrote, "when communists are faced with resolute, determined, and superior force, they usually retreat."[23] In such a sweeping comment Morison is in danger of using the same logic that asserts that all Orientals look alike. Such logic is useless for

Communists or any other group. Vietnam is a sad reminder that generalizations of that kind are unhappy compromises with truth. Recognition of the dangers of Communism as an ideology have seldom been satisfactorily separated from a nationalism which has implemented the "Third World." Ideological struggles are not only misleading, they are highly dangerous. With the inception of the atomic age ideological politics point the way to planetary suicide. FDR was somehow able to make the distinction. He unhesitatingly rejected the Communist ideology but he avoided allowing American diplomacy to be ensnared by a counter doctrinal rigidity. At Yalta FDR did not misjudge Communism; he misread persons and motives.

It must not be forgotten that Roosevelt utilized force in the national interest. Because we have for so long based our foreign policy upon the "Communist menace" theory, some very intelligent critics are prepared to reject all national use of strength and force. This could prove suicidal in a non-ideal world, and that extreme a response may be tantamount to insisting on government by the Sermon on the Mount, a patently absurd idea.

President Truman's intervention in Greece and Turkey seems, in retrospect, reasonable action, though at the time the *Christian Century* called it the beginning of a "long and blood-soaked road."[24] The editor was distressed at the decision to shore up rotting dictatorship. It was a valid point, one that should have been made. If the use of force in these two countries proved wise, it was not because one always uses force when facing the Communists, a kind of Pavlov reaction. Ideological diplomacy cuts off options and endangers the balance of reason in the world.

President Truman did not need to create this ideological scare as a by-product of legitimate foreign policy. In so doing he encouraged the rise of Senator Joseph McCarthy. Truman spoke in 1949 of the "false philosophy of communism" which created an East-West confrontation. Balance-of-power politics was abandoned for doctrine. Admittedly, the balance-of-power diplomacy had hardly been a smashing success, but at least it kept nations in touch with reality.

It is probable that the Truman position of identifying Communism as the world enemy of democracy was a categorical error which prompted much of the "brinksmanship" of the Eisenhower days. We cannot ascertain to what extent Mr. Truman was reacting to religious stimulus in his decisions, but he unfailingly employed religious symbols to support his actions. Prodded by his reading of the world situation, the Korean War became more than a police action; it became the battleground between good and evil. "The Korean War became the main catalyst of American military involvement in the Far East and Southeast Asia. Not only that; it prompted the Americans to become more deeply involved all over the world, wherever they saw, rightly or wrongly, a threat of Communist penetration or subversion."[25] Recent disclosures of official Pentagon documents have reinforced this conclusion, pinning the roots of the Vietnam struggle in the Truman administration.

It does not follow that a non-ideological foreign policy is isolationist or weak by nature. The opposite may be true if, in the fear of alien ideas, unwise decisions are triggered. The ideological battle often becomes an engagement between good and evil in a final Armageddon and in the process rational communication is eliminated. Everything from arms to butter becomes a tool in the doctrinal fight.

The myth that American operations are motivated unfailingly by humanitarian ideals requires reappraisal in the light of reality. This is particularly true in the area of foreign aid. The United States has pushed the selfless image until the nation seems to believe it. But if that be a true interpretation of motive, why did we feed starving inhabitants of India and pray for crop

When we seek to define it otherwise it becomes mere pious propaganda. Now, a realistic perspective does not vitiate the validity of foreign aid programs. It only says that our pride as a people can make these programs demonic.

No better evidence of "food diplomacy" could have been produced than the self-righteous reaction of the Administration to those nations which dared to express pleasure over the exclusion of Taiwan from the United Nations. Fortunately, the entire foreign aid package appears finally to be under scrutiny by Congress from a realistic rather than a moralistic perspective.

Truman often acted from instinct, and on many occasions he was vindicated in his decisions. He was in some ways a bridge between the New Deal and the age of Eisenhower. His emotions were with Roosevelt; his religious and ideological base was inclined toward Ike. While Truman fits Type B, his flexibility requires the restatement of the obvious: that all schemes are fluid. Nevertheless, Harry Truman stands as an advocate of the Puritan ethic and American "Messianism."

Toward the close of his eventful years in the White House, Truman saw the development of unbridled ideological warfare in this country, and he was powerless to contain it. Walter Lippmann supported Eisenhower in 1952 because he believed that only a Republican victory would halt the demagogue Joseph McCarthy. President Truman did not bow to the outrageous demands of the Wisconsin Senator but his own popular credentials were in serious disrepair as a result of scandals in the White House and the dismissal of General Douglas MacArthur. The MacArthur firing was opposed by 69 percent of the American public.

In all his actions Mr. Truman had a unique way of injecting religion into policy. From the earliest period of his administration he had requested prayer for his office. He was a member of the First Baptist Church of Washington which he attended on occasion, but it is probably stretching the point to say he on occasion, but it is probably stretching the point to say he attended with "unfailing regularity."[26] He did receive the praise of the religious press when he attended Sunday School in 1947. In a typical overstatement he was acclaimed for setting a good example for all citizens to follow.[27]

By 1949 Mr. Truman's religious zeal had become too much for the *Christian Century.* Speaking to a group of Anglican bishops, the President had stated that the Sermon on the Mount was what America was living by. The *Century* editor found it difficult to believe that the administration was trying to mobilize the nation for the Sermon on the Mount.[28] A week later the same editor suggested that Mr. Truman might consider pardoning the conscientious objectors still in prison since we were living by the Sermon. The following year the President reiterated his stand with remarks to a group of Lutherans when he said that the Sermon on the Mount was governing American policy in its leadership role over the moral forces of the world. He drew a sharp line of demarcation and said the Communists were evil because they did not believe in a supreme being. He did not comment upon the character of atheists who were American citizens.[29] After his election in 1948 Mr. Truman became more vigorous in painting the world in black and white terms, a tendency which seemed most apparent in his numerous appearances before religious gatherings during the fifties. The farther he moved from 1945 the more easily the President defined his policy as a religious crusade in a manner consistent with the Germans of the First World War when they inscribed "Gott mit uns" on their belt buckles.

Late in 1952, after the November election, Mr. Truman made a forceful presentation of his outlook on democracy and religion to a group of churchmen. He said: "Democracy is, first and foremost, a spiritual force, it is built upon a spiritual basis —and on a belief in God and an observance of moral principle. And in the long run only the church can provide that basis. Our

founder knew this truth—and we will neglect it at our peril."[30]
The President had laid the foundation for these remarks in two
speeches delivered in the previous year, one of which is the most
thorough expression of Truman's religious philosophy extant.
Some excerpts follow.

> . . . religion should establish moral standards for the conduct of
> our whole nation, at home and abroad. . . .
>
> For the danger that threatens us in the world today is
> utterly and totally opposed to all these things [spiritual values].
> The international Communist movement is based on a fierce and
> terrible fanaticism. It denies the existence of God and wherever
> it can it stamps out the worship of God. . . . Our religious faith
> gives us the answer to the false beliefs of Communism. . . . I have
> the feeling that God has created us and brought us to our present
> position of power and strength for some great purpose.[31]

The subliminal "Scripture" for this tying of religion and
democracy into a societal faith has been the Constitution.
Though a national cult be construed as multifaceted, the Constitution wears the aura of finality for all. Interestingly enough,
Thomas Jefferson would have rejected this development. "Jefferson blasted judicial review as 'the despotism of an oligarchy.'
Taylor's attack was even more vehement, and so was Van
Buren's, but in the end the work of Marshall flourished and the
symbolism of Court and Constitution became a national fetish."[32] Roosevelt's effort to "pack" the Court in the name of
the majority, a Jeffersonian ploy that backfired, provoked Herbert Hoover to thrust the following charge at his successor.

> It is the Supreme Court defending the people's rights and securi-
> ties guaranteed by the Constitution which time and again has
> protected the people from those who seek for economic power
> or political power or to suppress free worship and free thought.
> It is the people's rights that are endangered.[33]

The almost religious worship of the Court and Constitution in its adjudicative power symbolized an "ethical settle-

ment." When the Court interprets the political scripture in a symbolic fashion, the Jeffersonian liberals are made content. On the other hand, the conservative reacts with efforts to curb the Court, presently exemplified in the move of Senator Harry F. Byrd, Jr., to require, through constitutional amendment, review of all federal judges every eight years. Otherwise, he notes, there is no check on them at all. However, when the Court becomes restrictive and literalistic in its views, the liberal seeks redress through methods such as that of FDR in his attempt to pack the Court. Of course, by the nature of the appointment process the Court remains always out of phase with the pendulum behavior of the political persuasions of the other two branches of government. This was Roosevelt's problem and it has been Nixon's problem. If the Constitution is a kind of "civil scripture," then the Court is an "ecumenical council" that interprets the document by issuing doctrinal statements, i.e., its decisions.

The Supreme Court itself has powerful influence on American thought, but it is seldom popular. It is a "prophet without honor." When Americans determine to inject God into this political complexity in order to simplify by divine decree, the question is raised as to who is this God. Is he the selective God of judgment that inspired Wilson? Is he the God of business who rewards those who practice diligence as defined by Hoover? Is he the God of the universe whose benevolent plan may inspire all men as it did Roosevelt? Is he the friendly sovereign who has chosen America, blessed her, and given her a special mission as seen by Truman and Eisenhower? Just how is America to plumb the theological depths of her own variegated religious heritage? Beyond all these inquiries, it is never quite clear when religion is determining politics and when it is just the reverse. There was no one civil religion during the Truman era, but during the years that followed there was a major effort to subsume all traditions under one pious umbrella.

3 • PRAYER AND FEAR UNEQUALLY YOKED

> The pursuit of peace is at once our religious obligation and
> our national policy.
> —DWIGHT EISENHOWER

The election of Dwight Eisenhower and Richard
Nixon marked the end of an era and the total restoration of
American "Messianism." In this century, with the possible
exception of Wilson, no man in the presidency has received
more attention for his religion. In a somewhat mild and belated
repeat of the election of 1920, the citizenry selected a man who
incarnated their own idea of Deity. But the religion which Ike
brought to the White House was as humorless as the times that
inspired it. Yet, whatever its description there was religion in
abundance. Most scholars of American religion have taken a
hand at identifying the mood, and Will Herberg is a good
representative. Writing of the religion of the fifties he concluded:

> But it is a curious kind of religion. The very same people
> who are so unanimous in identifying themselves religiously, who
> are joining churches at an accelerating rate, and who take it for
> granted that religion is a "very important" thing, do not hesitate
> to acknowledge that religion is quite peripheral to their everyday
> lives; more than half of them quite frankly admit that their
> religious beliefs have no influence whatever on their ideas in
> economics and politics, and a good proportion of the remainder
> are obviously uncertain.[34]

It was the beginning of the time when laymen would in ever
increasing numbers scold the clergy for involving itself in matters other than spiritual, i.e., politics and social justice.

In 1952, shortly after his election, President Eisenhower
said, "Our government makes no sense unless it is founded in

a deeply felt religious faith, and I don't care what it is." Earlier, in 1948, the General had delivered himself of this sentiment: "I am the most intensely religious man I know. . . . Nobody goes through six years of war without faith. That does not mean that I adhere to any sect. A democracy cannot exist without a religious base. I believe in democracy."[35] What the new President wanted was to rally all "faiths" to endorse the American system as God's way.

Sociologist E. Digby Baltzell says, "President Eisenhower calmly reigned as representative of a generation still dominated by the Protestant establishment . . ."[36] That establishment had slowly eroded over the past half-century until it was transformed by mid-twentieth century into an essentially tripartite character.[37] It may be this transition in Protestantism that explains the revival mood of the fifties and the death of God of the sixties. The fear which the churches expressed over the death-of-God movement suggests the basic shallowness of the so-called revival of the previous decade.

Eisenhower was an almost perfect mirror of establishment religion, a domestic move to the right not dissimilar to the Harding-Coolidge era.[38] On the Sunday following his inauguration the President joined a sect, the Presbyterian Church in Washington. It was a natural middle-ground act for the President, one which, according to the *Chicago Tribune,* included baptism.

Dwight David Eisenhower was named for the well-known nineteenth-century evangelist Dwight L. Moody. The Eisenhowers of Abilene, Kansas, were members of a Mennonite sect which had its origins in the European Reformation. Their specific branch of this pacifist tradition was the River Brethren Church. Sometime around the turn of the century David's mother joined the Jehovah's Witnesses, suggesting a strong literalistic approach to the Bible. It seems that young David did not take to the pacifism of his heritage, for he entered the United States Military Academy in 1915. But the Witnesses' simplistic approach to the Bible left its impress on the youth. He did not again identify with a sect until 1953.

According to his own testimony Ike was a religious man during the Second World War. He exhorted his troops to fight for spiritual causes, and he proclaimed the Allied effort a crusade. He believed that democracy was founded upon biblical values with the spiritual conviction that each person has worth in the sight of God. He further identified democracy with the free enterprise system, so that his total religious orientation was in agreement with the fundamental dogma that problems are solved through virtue and hard work. To him paternalistic government, his term for collectivism, was a threat to freedom, although as President he certainly accepted the vast majority of the New Deal–Fair Deal legislation. Paul Hutchinson, in writing about the President's religion, said that Eisenhower believed that all would be well for a person if he would take the cards life dealt and play them properly.

For the General, a soldier and a clergyman were in the same business—defending the dignity of man and the glory of God. He was certain that the soldier could justify his presence on the battlefield as a service to God. Of course, this presumed he was a soldier in the right army. When Ike turned to his 1952 campaign crusade it was mobilized against moral corruption in government, lack of integrity and honesty. Eisenhower in all this was "fervent about vague religion."[39]

The song that inspired Ike's faith is described in these words by the President. "There was a song some years ago that made a great impression on me, and it has a title that has been rather a motto for me ever since I got into politics. And it was this: 'I Believe.' "[40] This faith in belief was an affirmation of cause and effect—"For every drop of rain that falls, a flower grows."

Eisenhower's conviction that man could trust in God and find repose was in keeping with the widespread revival of religion in America. The high priests of popular religion in the fifties were Norman Vincent Peale and Billy Graham. In associating with these men and others such as the popular preacher Ralph Sockman and the simplifier-theologian Elton Trueblood, Eisenhower touched the heartstring of the nation, which was in a religious mood. It was Ike who inaugurated the White House Prayer Breakfast, and it was he who sought to establish a national day of prayer. As Elmer Davis pointed out, religion and recreation were not far apart, for having called the nation to its knees in prayer on July 4, 1953, Eisenhower went fishing in the morning, played golf in the afternoon, and played bridge that night. The President opened his Cabinet meetings with prayer and was in many ways the pious center for the American public. The people liked what they saw and heard. They felt secure in the knowledge that their President was a man of prayer, concerned for the spiritual things of life. It never bothered the public that Ike experienced no such need for public display of religion when he was commanding the greatest army in modern history. The people seemed mesmerized by the Peale-Graham line interpreted through Dwight Eisenhower.

The cynic may properly assert that this was a religious facade, merely an aspect of presidential image building. But if Eisenhower was not a religious man, then neither were millions of citizens in this land. And that is a gross oversimplification. That it was not religion as a cutting edge but rather one based on the notion of divine destiny for the nation does not remove it from the category of the religious. It was the closest America had come to self-consciously establishing a civil religion. People felt better because the pledge of allegiance had the phrase "under God" added to it, though there might be some problem theologically in defining that amorphous deity. He was Graham's "God up there" to millions of Christians, Jews, and agnostics alike. Only a discerning minority, a small minority indeed, cried "Foul."

In his effort to make America pious, President Eisenhower had the support of Billy Graham. Mr. Graham had experienced little restraint in his criticism of President Truman, but with Ike, Billy Graham grew to be a national religious symbol. In 1953 Graham averred: "The overwhelming majority of the American people felt a little more secure realizing that we have a man who believes in prayer at the helm of our government at this crucial hour."[41]

Dwight Eisenhower was the marvelous champion of the Goldilocks Era, that time in our history when everything was "just right"—not too hot, not too cold. In spite of his generalized piety, Ike was nonetheless an establishment Protestant and tried to maintain things as they had been. While he was not an astute student of either history or religion, he had learned well the traditional Calvinist virtues. For foreign affairs he made doubly certain that these virtues would be observed.

It was acknowledged at the time and confirmed by historians that Eisenhower was not his own Secretary of State. John Foster Dulles, as Secretary, became the President's alter ego. Dulles *was* the Eisenhower administration as far as affairs abroad were concerned. He was a churchman of no mean achievement—a perfect blend of competence and morality which satisfied the nation, although his former colleagues in church ecumenical circles became bitterly disappointed in his performance.[42] Dulles provided the foreign policy and the President provided the charm in international diplomacy. History has not clearly defined the Eisenhower role in determination of policy, but it may have been more significant than many assumed at the time. In any event, the President respected his Secretary and trusted him implicitly. If as some now say, Ike was less ideologically disposed than Dulles, he never openly broke with his Secretary on issues.

John Foster Dulles, Princeton graduate, had worked on a Russian relief problem for Wilson in 1919. He was an experienced diplomat with wide practical knowledge, among the best qualified men ever to hold the office. He came to the post with the intertwined religio-political personality that satisfied the President and the nation.

"Mr. Dulles belongs to the company of those whose anti-Communism is a matter of absolute principle, not of practical realism, because his own faith is so closely bound up with the ideals of the American tradition. . . . he fails to perceive the relativity of these ideals. . . . this failure of insight is rooted in a faith which emphasizes the Law at the expense of the Gospel."[43] Thus wrote one of America's most competent Christian ethicists in 1958. Dulles was convinced that America had a mission in the world and that material prosperity had tempted her to give up that calling. He said in 1950: "As a nation, although still religious, we have lost the connexion between our religious faith and our practices. . . . We can no longer generate a spiritual power which will flow throughout the world. . . . We have no message to send to captive peoples to keep their faith and hope alive."[44] Some have complained that Mr. Dulles gave a little too much "message" to the Hungarians for the available support we would supply.

Dulles certainly seemed to equate western Christianity, in particular the United States, with God's will. God had given America a destiny over against atheistic Communism. At times his religious zeal on this matter was absolute, leaving the impression that the world was not big enough for the two—Christians and Communists. By injecting that doctrinaire note into his policies, Dulles aided in the creation of a surly mood in this nation toward all things Communist. This was transferred into many of the churches in the fifties.

Harvard Professor Crane Brinton was asked recently why Americans are "bugged" by Communism. His reply was instructive.

> In short, atheism, anticlericalism, and all the rest in this country has grown increasingly unpopular. Church attendance or at least some identification with church is great. Let's not go into the question of true Christianity, but we are a church-going

people and the Russians have clearly in the past and continue to persecute Christians and Jews as religious people.[45]

The fifties produced some of the most glaring examples of excess on the question of Marxism. The decade began with the conviction of Alger Hiss for perjury, and the terror was not clearly at an end until the censure of Senator Joseph McCarthy in 1954. Whereas President Truman had fought back, the new President was far more subservient to the Wisconsin witch-hunter. Senator Robert Taft of Ohio was Ike's legislative chief, and the Senator had encouraged McCarthy. Even in the 1952 campaign, Eisenhower, when touring Wisconsin, found it expedient to be on the same platform with Senator McCarthy. Further, he felt pressured to delete mention of George C. Marshall from his prepared text because McCarthy had said Marshall was subversive. To some impressionable college students, that was the first warning that Ike was not a moral giant replacing petty corruption. For the most part Eisenhower escaped to the high road of moralism, however, by delegating the Communist issue to his running mate, Richard Nixon.

While Secretary Dulles was an almost inflexible moralist, he was no bigot. He would have no part in the Joe McCarthy smear tactics. He transcended them. Actually, the President attempted the same thing with a modicum of success. When all effort to control McCarthy had failed and one of his aids blundered by accusing five thousand Protestant clergy of being "red" or "pink," it was Nixon who was given the task of axing the Senator.

Certainly the Dulles position appeared far more "centrist" in character as a result of the right-wing scare techniques and the investigations of the Wisconsin Senator. In many ways Dulles reminded one of Wilson, but unlike him, Mr. Dulles faced critical problems of life and death for the planet on a daily basis. Here inflexible moralism could become a dangerous attribute rather than an irritant upon which later historians might

"Quick, Men—Get That Bible Off The Shelves"
From *Herblock's Here And Now* (Simon & Schuster, 1955)

muse. Dulles created for the Eisenhower administration the image of fortress America, messianic beyond the days of Truman. America was in tune with the moral law of God and was to save the world with superior morality and strength. The strength was God's gift for the morality. In the fifties those nations that saw fit to chart a middle course were castigated by the administration, the press, and the public as dupes of Communist aggressors. The emerging Third World was not aided by Dulles, and many of its components still resent America. Prime Minister Nehru of India, a genuine friend and admirer of the United States, had an exceptionally difficult time with the hostile conservative press, which regularly viewed him as an opportunist milking American kindness while flirting with the enemy. Few recognized the "beam" in America's own eye.

It is difficult to explain all the reasons why Dwight Eisenhower captured the American people the way he did. He was, of course, a war hero, but it had been nearly eight years since V-E Day. He did have a certain natural charm which made him a likable candidate, but it was not exceptional. Until late in the game, neither party was clear as to his affiliation. His politics did not seem to matter. While he was the candidate of progressive Republicanism of the Lodge-Dewey variety, by the time he was elected the split with Taft had been healed. Ike did not appeal to the voters because of his political philosophy. Adlai Stevenson was never able to make a race out of the campaign simply because he was the only candidate with a philosophy of government. Again, it may be suggested that anyone could have taken the measure of the Democrats in 1952. But that does not explain the attachment to the candidate. Eisenhower did not possess the charisma of Roosevelt or Kennedy, or even Wilson. He was surely no orator.

Eisenhower conveyed integrity, old-fashioned honesty and decency. He was, the populace felt, a real American who projected the warmth and image that the majority saw in themselves. Ike did not, like FDR, move the country to reflect his personality. Rather, he reflected back to the people their own popular image of the nation. He exuded confidence to a conflict-weary people. "His genial character and transparent honesty inspired loyalty to himself and confidence in his administration."[46] He had a kind of generalized piety which made the country feel good. He brought piety to the Potomac.[47]

Eisenhower represented the secular religionist described by Will Herberg as "being serious about religion but not taking religion seriously." His sentiments were simple, and he appears from this vantage point to have done a remarkable job of creating an American religiosity that had precious little to do with either the Constitution or the Delcaration of Independence, not to mention the Bible. His was an administration of big business and his Cabinet appointments caused Adlai Stevenson to quip that the New Dealers had been replaced in Washington by the car dealers.

The White House religion, which so encouraged the nation in its piety and aided in the rise to prominence of Billy Graham as a political force, placed little emphasis on sect or faith commitment, only on a kind of divine feeling. It was the era of the "Man Upstairs" and prayer before college football games. The people felt quite self-righteous, though the fear of Communism and the "bomb" pervaded the fifties and Sputnik frightened the nation in 1957. For many, prayer was a substitute for thinking about problems. It was during the reign of Ike that the country came closer than ever before to establishing a civil religion. It would have been a modified Puritanism divested of ethical and theological content. There was a totally uncritical approach to the Bible, a fact which is attested by the various motion pictures of the period. Modern biblical scholarship was rejected or ignored. It was a decade of simplistic faith when Hollywood could market "Peter Marshall" and audiences would respond with tears and faith. It was a nostalgic effort to return to the old-time religion.

Then there was a Catholic.

I hope we shall never forget that we created this Nation, not to serve ourselves, but to serve mankind.
—WOODROW WILSON

V • The Twentieth Century Comes to the White House

1 • PRAGMATISM REVISITED

If we cannot now end our differences, at least we can help make the world safe for diversity.
—JOHN KENNEDY

The nation was told in the election campaign of 1960 that for the first time both major candidates were born in this century, and this was supposed to tell us something about the potential character of their administrations. The irony of history has within a decade placed both these young men in the White House, but has produced no radical political alterations. New style and verve to be sure, but in essentials the two men fit patterns long established in American presidential behavior. There were radical events and changes in the sixties, but the Presidents of that era were responding to those new crises in highly predictable fashion.

In many ways the sixties might justifiably be described as the twilight of the traditional church. There have been many periods in the history of the West when notable persons spoke of faith over against the institutional religion of the day. Nevertheless, the majority were satisfied to equate religion with faith and formalize that religion into particular structures. This establishment mentality, coupled with the great variety of religious traditions in colonial America, caused the evolution of pluralism in American religious history. The notion of pluralism was based upon the assumption of real loyalty to institutional sects within the society. Of course, in a true sense there is remarkable unity pervading the country religiously in spite of its almost fratricidal conflicts. The Judeo-Christian tradition has always been the foundation of religion in modern Western culture, and the phenomenal success of Billy Graham in moving from the "God in Christ" to the "God up there" lies in this unity. However, it has only been in this half century that Americans have become conscious of that unity, thereby shifting the pluralistic concept to the back burner. Perhaps now the pluralism appears unimportant in comparison with the newly discovered oneness. It presumes that creeds no longer matter. It is the real secularization of the nation.

The potential for this shift has always existed. Somehow, though Protestants have persecuted Catholics and both have had a turn at the Jews, an underlying unity has prevailed in the common acceptance of the Bible. The pluralism was only skin-deep, for we are expressing varieties of one culture, the Western European culture. Earlier generations made certain there would be no African culture by ruthlessly destroying any possibility of its survival among the slaves. It is this common culture which made it difficult for Americans to speak humanely about the Japanese during the Second World War, while seeking to find rationale for the Germans. Even during the conflict's bitterest days, there was among many citizens a kind of "Hogan's Heroes" attitude toward the Germans. When John Fitzgerald Kennedy took the oath of office he was nothing new to the

American scene, culturally or politically. He was Huck Finn come of age and accepted. Indeed, he embodied far more of the realities of the American present than had Eisenhower. The insertion of the Catholic question into the campaign was a predictable result of the sharp conflicts in our culture stemming from the Reformation. But the vast majority of American Protestants, even those who voted against him for religious reasons, knew John Kennedy was really "one of them." The Catholic issue was the result of a "family feud," but it was far from being a major religious fissure such as presently is visible between the cultures of Buddhism and Islam in India and Pakistan.

Of course, family feuds can prove fatal, and it is chilling to contemplate what might have been the psychological effects upon the nation had the razor-thin margin of 1960 gone the other way. In his book *Six Crises,* Richard Nixon notes that the movement of about 13,000 votes in key states would have elected him.[1] By so few was the Catholic matter laid to rest in this country.

We see now that the election of President Kennedy was not the final recognition of our pluralism; rather, it was the assertion that our pluralism was irrelevant. It was the death of pluralism as a political issue.

Eisenhower pietism was the last gasp of the Protestant era in America. And it was not to be replaced by another sectarian era; rather, it was determined that in the future doctrinal faith of no sect would control the ideals of the populace. Any further presidential efforts in that direction would be anachronistic. The imminent danger is a non-doctrinal civil religion as a substitute for the faded Protestant establishment. Such a course may only be effectively protested by the enunciation of the prophetic faith of the Judeo-Christian tradition. The voice may be that of unlikely prophets, such as Pierre Berton, who have a profound grasp of the nature of the Christian experience.[2]

It cannot be argued that President Eisenhower tried to

impose narrow interpretations of religion upon the public. But his mode of operation was out of the conservative Calvinism of the past, and he did identify in word and deed with the doctrinally oriented community. He gave the prestige of his office to the religion of an American past, the old-time religion with the regular virtues of hard work, diligence, and honesty. The hypocrisy of his creed never became evident to its supporters. They did not see that the hard work was by those who profited least from their own labors. Eisenhower would have no time for anyone who sought to prevent free election and voting. But many in this nation and abroad were saying that was not the essence of freedom. A new generation questioned the values of the old system with what it saw as an overabundance of self-righteousness and pride. Ike spoke of individualism and this "individualistic faith allowed little room for collective solutions to social problems or for collectivist interpretation of the social teachings of the Scriptures." His was a faith "more at home in Abilene, Kansas, at the turn of the century than in modern metropolitan America."[3]

Some have termed John Kennedy a "spiritually rootless modern man."[4] Others have spoken of him as secular man.[5] These references point to his unwillingness to adapt himself to institutional religion. JFK accepted religion as a part of his life, but his closest associate, Ted Sorenson, could say: "But not once in eleven years—despite all our discussions of church-state affairs—did he ever disclose his personal views on man's relation to God."[6] Sorenson also informs us that Kennedy cared "not a whit for theology." He apparently saw the Bible as a good source for quotations, but with no more reverence than he might have had for other great literature, and possibly less than he had for Jefferson. As one historian phrased it, he "wore his religion lightly."

John Kennedy spoke for a growing number in feeling that faith commitment is personal and that it may be annihilated by

institutionalizing it. While the older generation was warning
the younger to hold on to the religion of the churches, the youth
were leaving it in increasing numbers. While President Eisenhower could submit to Catholic pressure on birth control information distribution in 1959, John Kennedy could forthrightly
affirm the need to disseminate such information. JFK recognized political realities, but for him the church was not a legitimate pressure group. He did not succumb to ecclesiastical arm
twisting. In fact, old-line Protestants and Catholics were a great
deal closer together on their view of the old-time virtues than
were either to President Kennedy. He was not a Catholic President. He was a secular President who was affiliated with the
Catholic Church.

In the sixties intonings from the pulpit carried less and less
weight. In all periods of American history, from John Cotton
to Harry Emerson Fosdick and Reinhold Niebuhr, the nation
not only produced but heard spiritual leadership. It was not
always happily received but the force of personalities was felt.
College and university religious programs in the forties and
fifties brought "big names" theologically to packed houses. No
longer are there either packed houses or big names. When a
university director of religious affairs is torn between inviting
a prominent sociologist or a "relevant" comic book editor to
deliver lectures in religion, he knows he is living in 1972.
Though his crowds remain large, Billy Graham is a voice from
the past. Religion for the rising generation is, if anything, politics, economics, sociology.

The religious community has been talking largely to itself.
Religion is not selling well. We are experiencing a religious
recession. Such recession indicates something has changed, and
only the recognition of that important fact will allow a new
understanding to emerge. For one brief moment John Kennedy
may have shown the nation the way to challenge our rudderless
feeling, but Presidents Johnson and Nixon have sought to return to the old faith. It is not likely to succeed.

The current movement of the "Jesus People" is a tired retread of Moral Rearmament, likely another passing phase. To be sure, Jesus is a household word via "Superstar," but the religious significance of all this is dubious. At least one thing is becoming obvious. The church no longer has a corner on Jesus or the myths surrounding him. Cries of blasphemy will no longer silence the secularizing process. Effects upon the church's rituals and doctrines is still uncertain.

John F. Kennedy demonstrated early that trait of character which placed him in the category with Franklin D. Roosevelt. His election to the United States Senate in 1952 coincided with the severest outbreak of anti-Communism under the leadership of Senator McCarthy. Evidence is abundant to prove that John's father, Ambassador Joseph Kennedy, was a strong admirer of McCarthy. The Senator's brother Robert was on McCarthy's staff. Again, Joe McCarthy was a Catholic and, therefore, in the popular mind associated with other Catholic politicians. Yet John Kennedy, making the commitment that was to mark him through the rest of his life, rejected McCarthyism. While he provided no courageous leadership, leaving that to men like Lyndon Johnson, there is little question that JFK had determined upon opposition to McCarthy before he was stricken with illness and hospitalized. He was there immobile during the debate on the censure motion in November of 1954. Theodore Sorenson takes full responsibility for the failure to record a vote from JFK. He felt Kennedy was too ill to be consulted on the matter.

Senator John Kennedy suffered from the same malaise that afflicted most of his senatorial colleagues of the early fifties— cooperation with smear by silence. For this he deserves neither more nor less criticism than the rest of the Senators, liberal and conservative, who failed to follow the lead of Margaret Chase Smith, who had early issued a stinging indictment of McCarthy's methods. But Kennedy's commitment to liberty and freedom would not allow him to follow the natural course of supporting a family friend who was riding a tremendous wave of popular support. And it was Jack Kennedy who saw to it that Dr. J. Robert Oppenheimer, victim of vicious McCarthy attacks, was restored to official favor.

One might anticipate that a Catholic as President would be, if possible, more of a crusader against Communism than Secretary Dulles. Kennedy was, however, like FDR, a pragmatist rather than an idealist or dogmatist. He was able to assess problems of his office from a non-ideological frame of reference.

JFK was not bound by doctrine in either religion or politics. He built upon the insight of FDR. The thirties, as Digby Baltzell interprets them, "witnessed the complete triumph of naturalistic relativism over transcendental absolutism; theology was replaced by anthropology; and universalism of the inner consciences of men gave way before the particularistic conditioning of the external environment."[7] While this is an overstatement of the case, the movement away from absolutism to relativism in political decision making was important. And the first Catholic to be President was a "relativist-realist."

Jack Kennedy was not a new breed of politician, but he most certainly was a new breed of Catholic politician. Father Andrew Greeley has recently written: "The best of the young Catholic laity today seem to be much like John Kennedy in their lack of interest in the internal affairs of the Church."[8] Part of the reason for this sentiment, prevalent among thinking young Protestant laymen as well, lies in the refusal of the old guard to allow full and free participation in the internal affairs of government and policy. It is probable that much of the ultraconservative opposition to Kennedy in 1960 was far more interested in establishing ties between church and state than JFK was. They merely wanted their kind of church control. And had those same people known Kennedy's type of faith, they would have opposed him as being a humanist.

One further observation is important. In 1960 there were

some who were honestly disturbed by the pronouncements of the Vatican on church and state and were fearful of the effect that these doctrines might have on a young President. Their concern was based upon earlier papal decrees and, though, in retrospect, the fears were groundless, it is important to distinguish these persons from the fulminating fanatics who sought to impose permanent Protestant control in the nation. The former were sincere Americans who voted their political consciences with the feeling that while the Constitution clearly did not preclude a Catholic from being President, neither did it require that they vote for one. It would be foolish, in view of our present thesis, to say that a man's religion is irrelevant to his public performance. And if it is not irrelevant, then it is a legitimate political consideration.

As we have already seen, the position of the Catholic Church on Communism could not have been clearer. FDR had felt this when he made efforts to soften Pope Pius XII on the question of dealing with the Soviet Union. The antics of Joe McCarthy did nothing to allay the impression that Catholics were monolithic on that subject. Atheistic and anti-church, Communism was the mortal enemy of the faithful. The Catholic position seemed not very different from what Senator Eugene McCarthy described as the "moralistic and ideological" approach of John Foster Dulles.[9]

But JFK came in the tradition of Pope John XXIII rather than Pius XII. On April 20, 1963, President Kennedy commented upon John XXIII's encyclical "Pacem in Terris." After commending the "penetrating analysis of today's problems," he said: "As a Catholic I am proud of it; as an American I have learned from it. . . . We are learning to talk the language of progress and peace across the barrier of sect and creed."[10] Less than eight months later both the eighty-one-year-old Pope and the forty-six-year-old President were gone. The remarkable coincidence of these two figures on the world scene was highly significant. In fact, JFK was so much in the vanguard that he seems to have felt that some of the Catholic hierarchy in America were out to defeat him in 1960. He was the wave of the future in American Catholicism so ably championed in earlier days by *Commonweal* and certain social-minded priests. This gave him trouble with the traditional stance of his church. In that light he "did not seem to perceive any connection between the teachings of his religion and his social and political commitment, nor much relationship between the morality of his Church and the problems he faced in the world's most important office."[11]

John Kennedy posed a bigger problem for the Church than it could have imagined in 1960, the problem of its own credibility. For the new President, piety and faith were cut loose from institutional ceremony and form. His moral decisions were not a result of strict rearing to conform with some religious doctrinal position. He could hardly deny that the great traditions of his nation and his culture, not to mention Harvard, were weighted with the baggage of Christianity, but he moved freely with the notion that faith is a private matter woven from the fabric of human experience. His concern for democracy and freedom was extricated from the cocoon of ideological form, so he became possessor of far greater options in dealing with matters of national import.

Kennedy's speeches indicate a real concern to maintain the strength of the country. There was never any question about his devotion to the national interest. He was impressed more than most Presidents by the glory and pomp of the military, and it was he who created the ill-fated Green Berets. Like any man he did not consistently move in one direction. But the total impact of his comments and actions reminds one of FDR. While this is due largely, I believe, to a common Anglo-Catholic tradition, it is also true that the influence of the patrician East was upon them both.

Communism was to both FDR and JFK a real threat but never a monolith. In 1959 Kennedy asserted that the problem of recognition of Communist China was not a moral issue.[12] He was able to view the China question expurgated of the Dulles dogma. At the same time his realism guided him away from naive credulity respecting Communist ideology. As a political practitioner he was of the middle way. Now, some eight years after his death, his nation is far closer to his rational dealing with China.

If the words of Tom Wicker are accurate that "one finds no reason to doubt that religious belief and discipline had no effect whatever upon his Presidential conduct and judgment,"[13] the indictment is upon the Judeo-Christian complex that nurtured him. Of course, Wicker is thinking primarily of institutional religion, rather than belief. Nevertheless, Kennedy's moral strength, his humanism, did have other roots than traditional religion. It was history that moved this man, and the ideas which he cherished were from Jefferson and Lincoln. These men, like JFK, had their own religious sensitivity that affected their writing and thinking, but the result was humanism.

John Kennedy had learned that religion is a wellspring rather than a flag to be waved. Like his predecessors in office, he quoted Lincoln and Jefferson, but with a difference. To JFK these men were not saints to be revered. They were persons with ideas to share. Their insights fascinated his facile mind and so their effect was germinal. Kennedy's faith was filtered through history. Unlike many who had preceded him, his historical sensitivity had not made him a student of the Bible. He did not, as FDR had, quote extensively from Scripture. He was a man who discovered his own principles rather than having received them prepackaged. John Kennedy was the most adequate representative of the "New Morality" yet to appear on the American political scene.

Even holding his enlightened view of Communist ideology, JFK was not protected from disaster. This is painfully shown by the Bay of Pigs incident, and it is clear from the television debates of the 1960 campaign that Kennedy took a hard line on the Cuban problem. He was critical of Eisenhower for allowing Castro to come to power.

On the Berlin crisis and the Cuban missile encounter, Kennedy was more creative in his thinking and acting. On Berlin he was described by the *Christian Century* as having exhibited "firmness and restraint." In 1963 the President told an American University audience in a crucial speech that the key to peace was "mental disarmament." He said, in sharp contrast to the rationale for the First World War, we needed to make the world "safe for diversity." The measure of JFK's success is the present nature of Soviet-American relations.

William V. Shannon, responding to recent detractors of JFK, painted a fine portrait of the man in *The New York Times* for October 19, 1971. "Throughout his Administration, whether he was dealing with Congress or Khrushchev, with Southern racist Governors or steel company executives, Kennedy followed a consistent pattern of trying to narrow differences, to conciliate rather than confront, to seek face-saving compromises." Shannon makes a strong case for the proposition that above all else this talented man was a "peace-maker."

Kennedy applied strength without ideological fear to the two major crises that confronted his administration and forced the opposition to admit to itself and to the world that it could not hide behind its own ideology. JFK robbed the Communist nations, most particularly Russia, of their most devastating asset, the myth that Communism was a monolith. He was able to accomplish this because he rejected American "Messian-ism." It seems clear that John Kennedy was affected by his religious tradition in such a way as to see beyond national interests, and at the same time he was free enough to reject the ecclesiastical concerns with ideology which had so afflicted the hierarchy. His religion did for him what the Episcopal tradition had done for Roosevelt. It made them free men. Religion was personal, so there was no need of conflict between it and political action. It became a personal ethical gauge.

The "via media" was a valuable legacy of the Kennedy years. The avoidance of "Messianism" allowed a more intelligent appraisal of the options even in the Cuban missile crisis. This is in stark contrast with the Johnson Vietnam policy which led the President to go so far as to charge that the opposition in this country to his policy was soft on Communism.[14] The ironic quality of history is often intriguing. It had been Lyndon Johnson who recommended Senator Fulbright as Secretary of State to the Kennedy administration. One wonders about the policies of this government during the sixties had that suggestion been followed. Fulbright sounded the Kennedy thesis in the *Arrogance of Power.*

> And maybe—just maybe—if we left our neighbors to make their own judgments and their own mistakes, and confined our assistance to matters of economics and technology instead of philosophy, maybe then they would begin to find the democracy and the dignity that have largely eluded them, and we in turn might begin to find the love and gratitude that we seem to crave.[15]

A seasoned diplomat recently observed in conversation that if America would concentrate more upon being a model and less upon making "model democratic" nations, the world would be far better served.

As early as 1955 John Kennedy was moving toward the presidential goal. That was the year of his *Profiles in Courage.* In the closing chapter Kennedy wrote: "A man does what he must—in spite of personal consequences, in spite of obstacles and dangers and pressures—and that is the basis of all human morality."[16] Human morality is not, JFK recognized, love of people first. It is motivated by love of self. Speaking of the men whom he had sketched as demonstrating courage, he said:

> On the contrary it was precisely because they did *love themselves*
> —because each one's need to maintain his own respect for himself was more important to him than his popularity with others
> —because his desire to win or maintain a reputation for integrity and courage was stronger than his desire to maintain his office
> —because his conscience, his personal standard of ethics, his integrity or morality, call it what you will—was stronger than the pressures of public disapproval—because his faith that *his* course was the best one, and would ultimately be vindicated, outweighed his fear of public reprisal.[17]

Kennedy went on to say that as politicians they sometimes sought to "wring" advantage out of the course they had chosen and this was right for them to do as politicians. This self-confidence was later noted by Tom Wicker when JFK was in the White House. Kennedy demonstrated in his manner the self-assurance of Winston Churchill, who, when informed that his party had made him Prime Minister, sighed with relief in the knowledge that the nation was then in good hands. While Mrs. Franklin Roosevelt lamented at the Democratic Convention in 1960 that it was too bad Kennedy did not possess some of the courage about which he had written so eloquently, she could not foresee the shaping of the man in his new responsibilities. Her words were reminiscent of those written by Walter Lippmann about her husband in 1932.

Carrying, as he did, the inner light theory of ethics and morality, it is probable that John Kennedy could never have become doctrinaire about Communism. He was most concerned that religion not become a tool of the Cold War. To a Prayer Breakfast crowd imbued with Billy Graham politics he said in 1961: "I do not regard religion as a weapon in the Cold War."[18] At the same affair a year later he returned to this theme

From *Straight Herblock* (Simon & Schuster, 1964)

in almost identical words: "I do not suggest that religion is an instrument of the Cold War."[19]

Perhaps his own church, which had such a major part in the defeat of his domestic legislation in 1961, never fully understood the kind of man they had given to the nation. With his grasp of the democratic process, Kennedy had finally set Roman Catholics free from their imposed ethnic bondage and "Americanized" them. Andrew Greeley saw JFK as a "doctor of the Church." But he felt "American Catholicism's inability to respond to the phenomenon of John Kennedy in a more imaginative and creative way must be marked as a tragic failure. And by his relative indifference to what he presumably deemed the trivial internal concerns of Catholicism, JFK sat in judgment on this failure, without meaning to do so."[20]

Often it is lamented that we do not produce the kind of leadership which once was a hallmark of this nation. We no longer have Jeffersons and Franklins, Madisons and Adamses, we are told. I think rather that, whereas in the eighteenth century a man's ability was credential enough to give him opportunity for leadership, today the institutionalized nature of our society precludes the rise of men of high quality. The system rewards mediocrity. The quality that characterized the great men of the eighteenth century was a sterling intellect coupled with a drive to lead. They did not agree with one another but they respected each other's ability. In modern times, Roosevelt and Kennedy sought to utilize the best intellectual resources of the nation, and for it they were ridiculed and the intellectual became the "egghead." An army may travel on its stomach but a civilization moves on its mental and cultural power, and as a nation this is the faith we have misplaced—a tradition of the mind and a respect for ideas.

2 • WAR ON POVERTY BECOMES POVERTY OF WAR

But we are not about to start another war and we're not
about to run away from where we are.
                                                 —LYNDON JOHNSON

Lyndon Baines Johnson was a remarkable product of
Texas, but in most respects he is quite typical of the area. Eric
Goldman believes that the very locale of his birth tended to
nurture in him a superpatriotism with respect to foreign in-
volvements. In contrast, the international flavor of Kennedy
and Roosevelt is in a degree explicable by their birthplaces, both
on the East Coast. The heartland mentality toward Europe is
in marked contrast with that along the Atlantic shore. Mid-
America has consistently been the seat of isolationism and enthusiastic patriotic fervor. In spite of having been tutored by
FDR and having served in the Kennedy administration, Johnson was, nevertheless, demonstrably uneasy around foreign dip-
lomats and tended to refer all these persons, where possible, to
Secretary of State Dean Rusk.[21]

Not only was Lyndon Johnson a son of Texas, he was the
recipient of the standard Protestant upbringing of that state. He
had roots in Baptist and Disciples of Christ traditions. More
than most sections of the country, Protestantism of the Southwest tends to blend with the local culture. Any observer of
religious activities in Texas can attest to the influence of that
state's social structure and mores upon the institutions of religion. North Texans are Baptists and Disciples in overwhelming
numbers. The Disciples represent a mid-nineteenth-century
fragmentation of Baptists, and the two denominations have
similar ritual and theology. The Disciples have their largest

Southern representation in Texas, and Texas Christian University is a result of their stewardship. There are more Baptists in Texas than in any other state in the Union.[22]

Denominations are usually mirrors of the culture in which they are born. Participants in each religious sect tend to absolutize their tradition as the New Testament one, but in reality the Baptist or Disciple of Virginia or Texas will display in his religion what he construes as best in his sectional culture. This is one major explanation for inflated church rolls and a silence of prophetic voice. One of the most obvious and common aspects in all Southern states is the appeal of gospel songs and emotional hymns. In fact, this has even cut across racial lines. The tragedy of our culture has been that this community of appeal could not be transferred to content, and as a result those persons who sing "How Great Thou Art" are unable to join with those who cry "We Shall Overcome." The singers have been divided along racial lines, producing two distinct cultures in the South with one type of worship. And bound to the society as it was, Protestantism lacked vigor and vitality respecting political and social issues. Southern politicians became extreme caricatures of the region. Southern churches emphasized salvation of the soul and individual responsibility before God. The church did not find a way of making that faith relevant to societal needs any more than did the politicians who represented the section in Congress. The exceptions were few and Lyndon Johnson was one of them. He was bigger than the culture and the religion that spawned him. Thus his rousing address to Congress in 1966 did attempt to heal the division of race when he thundered to that august assembly, "We shall overcome." At this, even the most sophisticated liberals and intellectuals felt a chill up their spines.

President Johnson's administration must be divided into two parts—before and after the escalation in Vietnam. In the period from November 1963 until spring 1965 he was close to

THE AGONY AND THE ECSTASY

From *The Herblock Gallery* (Simon & Schuster, 1968)

an approximation of the American version of the universal man. He grasped the reins of government firmly and, certainly in the early days, determined to implement the stalled domestic program of his assassinated predecessor. What Kennedy might never have accomplished, Johnson achieved. It was not, of course, all due to his masterful talent in congressional persuasion, but the reputation grew that he was unbeatable in legislative struggles. He got the economic and social reforms so desperately needed by the nation and so dear to the heart of Jack Kennedy. Education finally received the funding it had long required, and the Civil Rights Bill of 1964 is a permanent monument to Johnson's commitment to equality under the law. He won the admiration of many skeptical liberals who watched with admiration his amazing progress. Consensus became a household word, and it appeared that the President was on his way to the most revolutionary administration in our century.

Then came Vietnam.

Lyndon Johnson is the grandson of a Baptist minister and is imbued with all the classic traditions of the Southwest. Those who have known him best find it difficult to pinpoint what he might think concerning personal religious faith. He is certainly an outwardly religious man, quoting appropriately from the Bible as occasion requires. In 1964 while speaking to a group of Baptists, he said that religion must always play a part in all our national decisions. He did not specify what role, but he was speaking concerning the civil rights legislation as he argued, "social problems are moral problems."[23]

If religious doctrine meant little to LBJ during his public life, he was certainly not anti-religious. While he took religion of the church in a rather conventional way, what Bellah described as the civil religion meant a great deal to him. He had certain values, chief among them being freedom. He "spoke the word with emotion."[24] He had an ardent sense that there was, in every decision to be made, a "right thing to do." His personal

American credo came from many years of strong feeling about the nation, with the full consciousness that history was looking over his shoulder.

President Johnson was an admirer of Franklin Roosevelt and had deep respect as well for Harry Truman. Apparently he did not care about Wilson, whom he felt was too rarified and "priggish." As to JFK, it seems doubtful that one can speak exactly about his attitude but clearly he had quite different reactions to Robert and John. Finally, LBJ had an appreciation of the administration of Eisenhower, under whom he served as majority leader in the Senate. This mixture of responses is sufficient to indicate the "consensus man." But he was not alone eclectic. His was a powerful personality with numerous dimensions of his own.

It does not appear that Johnson used religion cynically, though use it he surely did. He did not attend church regularly, yet he seems to have respected those who did. While his conventional attitude toward institutional religion led him to accept Billy Graham and the Prayer Breakfast, he did not appear moved by that form of piety. Mrs. Johnson has several references to Graham in her recent book on the White House years that indicate a family friendship which included conversation and games.[25] The First Lady was particularly struck with a projected Graham crusade in the South and the new declaration on race by the evangelist. At the same time she seemed cool to the idea of a White House religious service projected by Nixon and Graham. The publication of the Johnson memoirs comes too late for assessment here. It should prove beneficial in filling out the portrait of personal religion of the former President.

The heartland Calvinism, filtered through Texas culture, did finally capture the man when Vietnam became his major problem. On the Sunday after the assassination Mr. Johnson met with Ambassador Lodge for a briefing on Vietnam, a meeting that Kennedy had planned. As new evidence continues to filter through to the American public it remains altogether uncertain to what extent Vietnam may have become an obsession with LBJ early in his presidency. As he moved deeper and deeper into the morass, he began to marshal arguments to support his policy, and as involvement grew he became more convinced that he was morally right. He showed less concern over what the public wanted and more concern about what was "right" in his eyes. He combined practical judgments with an American credo of freedom. He coupled this with an extreme "Messianism." The President tried to justify the war as a struggle for freedom, a point that has a hollow ring in light of recently published documents. He piously berated Barry Goldwater in the 1964 campaign and spoke very morally about the fact that we had already lost 190 men in the war and that escalation could mean the loss of 190,000. Evidence now indicates that he expected to expand the war in 1965 and was fully aware of this when he campaigned in 1964. If this is indeed the case, his blindness on American commitment in Vietnam led him to clothe his "Messianism" in piously misleading language.

As the noose of Vietnam tightened, LBJ became a crusader for a righteous cause against the powers of compromise and sellout. During the fall of 1967 he stormed the country with oratory, attacking his critics almost to the point of calling them traitors. And after that foray who can forget the bitter engagement between "mitre and sceptre" that occurred in Williamsburg, Virginia, in the ancient Bruton Parish Church, the church of Washington, Mason, Henry. A minister not known locally for his exciting behavior and his leadership among the clergy, used his sermon to question the President. Many asked, "Can the President have no peace from his critics even in church?" The inquiry simply pointed to the dilemma of the church in modern times. It has become the realm of the predictable and the safe. As national piety grew, desire for a "safe" clergy increased, a clergy unresponsive to social and political ills. Mr.

Johnson had sought to find in that church attendance a fitting conclusion to a speaking tour which invoked the god of war against the "timorous" critics who would counsel restraint in Vietnam. And with that incident in Williamsburg, somehow Mr. Johnson's religious crusade for his policies began to falter. By April of 1968 he was out of the political picture, largely a victim of his own ideological insistence that the war was just, being fought for just reasons. He would not countenance another Munich.

The facade that covered the Johnson rationale for the Vietnam conflict was far less sophisticated than that which shrouds the Nixon policy. The unvarnished patriotism was an honest function of the man, but the "Messianism" was the same. James Reston caught the image of LBJ in a 1965 article.

> He believes in the hard doctrines of John Calvin and individual responsibility, and now that the planned deficit and the tax cut have increased prosperity, he even believes a little in John Maynard Keynes. He is fiercely patriotic. He genuinely believes that God looks out for Uncle Sam. He has no doubt that this nation was set apart to achieve good and noble purposes . . .[26]

Yet Reston did not see Johnson as a deeply religious man, and he noted that LBJ was little changed in his attitude toward life after his severe heart attack in 1955. Most competent observers agree in saying that Johnson believes in the myths of the nation. "He believes in the American system."[27] Commenting on newly released information concerning the war in June of 1971, Reston expressed another sentiment when he wrote: "The documents prove once more that truth is the first casualty of war and that war corrupts good men."[28]

If Johnson's "Messianism" seems more homey, more down-to-earth, it is due to a lack of conscious ideological substructure. Because the ideology was so buried, the President was probably hard pressed to understand the dynamics of the Eugene McCarthy attack during the winter and spring. For the

President it was a matter of national honor and patriotism. As one looks back to the 1964 victory over an absolute ideologue the present plight of Johnson caught by hidden presuppositions becomes more pathetic. LBJ was a kind of negative replay of Wilson, stumping the country for a righteous cause. Now war rather than peace was the issue, but the silent partner in both instances was American missionism abroad. Johnson's cultural and spiritual past surfaced on international affairs and the results were all too plain. And they were as obvious in his dealing with the Dominican Republic as they appeared in Vietnam.

3 • NORMALCY REVISITED?

> Selflessness is the greatest asset an individual can have.
> —RICHARD NIXON

Richard M. Nixon may be the most self-consciously religious man to enter the White House since Wilson. Detractors who have referred to Mr. Nixon as a heartless and ruthless pragmatist have, I believe, largely missed the man in their appraisal. Obviously, President Nixon has an acute political sense and is able to move quickly for political advantage, but the matter of motivation is extremely important. Is he impelled only by base motives of pride and lust for power? Many have so asserted. However, the total picture of the man will not support that judgment. If it is true that the American public and press expect a President suddenly to transcend his humanity when he assumes the cloak of office, that same public and press are equally accustomed to judge a President as if he lacked the slightest bit of human complexity. Man can be

"Everybody Happy?"
Copyright 1971 by Herblock in *The Washington Post*

caricatured to such an extent that he ceases to be human, thus distorting his true nature. In portraying Mr. Nixon in a sinister guise, critics fail to do justice to the total human being and to history.

President Nixon is known to have a personal friendship with Billy Graham. Some claim that Graham is to be thanked for Mr. Nixon's decision to run in 1968.[29] It is also true that Nixon has an attachment to Norman Vincent Peale. Graham and Peale marked out the major extremes in popular religion during the fifties. The underlying unity between *World Aflame* and *The Power of Positive Thinking* has been conservatism in economics and politics, something they both shared with Richard Milhous Nixon. Peale and Graham endorse the essentials of American "Messianism." They support the traditional religious establishment in the nation and the values of self-discipline, achievement, individualism, and thrift.

Peale trades heavily on the pseudo-psychological ideas of "peace of mind" and self-understanding. His position on religion conjures up the "Gospel of Wealth" theology of the previous century. In this schizophrenic world, wholeness is to be achieved by self-acceptance. As a self-made man, Mr. Nixon must have been attracted by the Peale "logic" and by his endorsement of a national purpose based upon God's will. Expurgated of theology, which is not really important to either man, Graham and Peale sound very much alike on this subject.

And if Nixon discovers peace of mind with Norman Vincent Peale, he may have discovered peace with God through Billy Graham. Nixon's strong ideological bent against Communism had early expressed itself in the Alger Hiss case and the 1950 Senate campaign against Mrs. Douglas. Mr. Graham's words are and have remained compatible with the Nixon thesis. "Above all we are faced with the mighty force of Communism —the greatest, most well organized and outspoken foe of Christianity that the church has confronted since the days of pagan Rome."[30] Nixon would know God by fighting his battles here on earth. The face of the monolith slowly changed over the years from Russia to China, and we have not as yet had sufficient time to assess Graham's response to the new China policy. In the past, in any event, President Nixon has found in Billy Graham the spiritual arm for his anti-Communism. This has been coupled with a strong assertion of the traditional virtues which make us a "holy people."

Richard Nixon's entire political career has been predicated on a hard line against Communism. In his 1962 book he spoke of the Communist threat as "indivisible," "universal," and "total." He concluded by stating that Communism is doomed to failure because it is contrary to man's nature. "Man needs God, and Communism is atheistic."[31] The White House has altered this outlook more in the past three years than one might have supposed. The principle of American righteousness remains for Nixon, but the practical application of world policy has shown subtle changes. He has, for one thing, dropped the doctrinaire approach to China.

Richard Nixon the diplomat and author wrote an article in 1967 for the scholarly community in *Foreign Affairs.* It was an enlightened presentation entitled "Asia After Viet Nam." In it Nixon did not rattle the saber or speak of *the* Communists; rather, he discussed in reasoned fashion some alternatives in Southeast Asia. In what now must be seen as a forerunner of the "ping-pong diplomacy" of the spring of 1971, Nixon asserted:

> Dealing with Red China is something like trying to cope with the more explosive ghetto elements in our own country. In each case a potentially destructive force has to be curbed; in each case an outlaw element has to be brought within the law; in each case dialogues have to be opened; in each case aggression has to be restrained while education proceeds; and, not least, in neither

case can we afford to let these now self-exiled from society stay exiled forever. We have to proceed with both an urgency born of necessity and a patience born of realism, moving step by calculated step toward the final goal.[32]

Of course the words of this statement still carry the implications of a "white man's burden," but they are a far cry from the days of Alger Hiss. It does not appear from the data available that Nixon actually changed between 1962 and 1967; rather, circumstances affected his options. Nixon does not think he changed. In 1970 he said: "Then [post-war period] we were confronted by a monolithic Communist world. Today, the nature of that world has changed—the power of individual Communist nations has grown, but international Communist unity has been shattered. Once a unified bloc, its solidarity has been broken by the powerful forces of nationalism."[33] Of course, it was men like Richard M. Nixon, and including him, who perpetrated the monolith myth more than twenty years ago. It was John Kennedy who defused that explosive topic and Nixon, though an ideologue, is no fool. He recognizes that American moralism and "Messianism" are going to have to seek alternative paths for the seventies.

In the issue for the week of December 20, 1971, *Newsweek* magazine had an incisive paragraph in its lead story about the India-Pakistani confrontation which identified the Nixon personality and dilemma exceptionally well.

From Woodrow Wilson to Lyndon Johnson, American Presidents have tended to approach foreign policy like missionaries on a moral crusade. But after Vietnam, Richard Nixon was left with little choice but to cool the self-righteous rhetoric. Last week, however, Mr. Nixon suddenly appeared to revert to past Presidential form. Confronted with another faraway Asian war where, this time, no American troops were involved and no vital American interests were at stake, the President curiously decided it was time for a bit of old-fashioned sermonizing.

The question of vital interest could well be debated, but the description of President Nixon at home in the messianic role is most instructive for prognosticators of future international relations.

President Nixon has *not* abandoned the messianic role of the nation. In 1969, shortly after this country had successfully reached the moon, the President told a group of foreign exchange students that "any culture which can put a man on the moon is capable of gathering all the nations of the earth in peace, justice and concord." Reinhold Niebuhr saw in this statement a categorical error typical in the West, that of identifying the self with the mind, creating an ideology and ignoring human ambitions, pride, and fears. Niebuhr concluded by saying that "an ideology is, in fact, a corruption of the reasoning process in the interest of self, individual or collective."[34] The ideological assumption of the "American Century" is at the heart of Mr. Nixon's total being. In shifting from the all-out fear of a Communist monolith Nixon has not forsaken his principles, and those principles still enervate his understanding of the American democracy.

Even the statement quoted above from *Foreign Affairs* is full of the messianic approach to international diplomacy. While Nixon's choice of the ghetto analogy was unfortunate as well as revealing, at least it did not assume, as many conservatives do, that the ghetto is the seedbed of Communism. At best the article made an invidious comparison due to Nixon's presuppositions.

The Nixon view of the national mission has not changed from 1960. "We must have a great goal. We also believe that in the great field of ideals that we can lead America to the victory for freedom . . . it is essential that we extend freedom, extend it to all the world."[35] In November of 1969 the President said:

> I know it may not be fashionable to speak of patriotism or national destiny these days, but I feel it appropriate to do so on this occasion . . . [because] the wheel of destiny has turned so that any hope the world has for the survival of peace and freedom will be determined by whether the American people have the moral stamina to meet the challenge of free world leadership.[36]

This assumption of a destined role is consistent with Nixon's Puritan beginnings. Religion is no small factor in forming character and character is primary in leadership. The binding of the destiny of the nation to moral insight is boldly stated on the jacket of a recent volume on presidential religion. "No one can read this book without reflecting on the relationship between responsibility and reverence, religion and national destiny."[37] The author makes it more explicit when he writes: "As one studies the lives of the presidents it would seem as though Providence had conspired to give them religious associations."[38] Richard Nixon finds agreement with this view. In 1969 he endorsed the Billy Graham remark that all Presidents "had left the presidency with a very deep religious faith."[39]

Richard M. Nixon was born into a Quaker home in the year 1913, in the area of Whittier, California. The records support the oft-repeated remark by Mr. Nixon that he was reared as a devout Quaker. He was the second person of that tradition in the White House in less than fifty years. When Herbert Hoover took office the *Christian Century* raised some question about his faith, remarking that Hoover was the first man in the White House who had a different religion. This was hardly the case, but the point was that no ideological pacifist had ever held the office. The *Century* did not oppose Hoover, but only asked how it would affect his performance of duty. Apparently it had no deleterious effect on the nation, though if held sincerely it must have influenced Hoover's thought.

Hoover was never very outspoken on the Quaker influence, but the attitude of Mr. Nixon is another matter.

In an interview with C. L. Sultzburger of *The New York Times* in March of 1971 President Nixon said:

> The older a nation and a people become the more they become conscious of history and also of what is possible. Now I will explain to you what I mean. I rate myself as a deeply committed pacifist, perhaps because of my Quaker heritage from my mother. But I must deal with how peace can be achieved and how it must be preserved.

In that same interview Mr. Nixon returned to the "selfless" image of America. He said: "We had fought four wars, selflessly and for no gain." Again Nixon, speaking of world peace, said it will not be the kind of peace that was "the dream of my Quaker youth." He protested that our role as world leader was thrust upon us and that we are a selfless nation that merely wants to do the right thing. Finally, he closed the interview with the following revealing words: "After all, if we manage to improve the environment and living conditions in this country we must also assure that we will be around to enjoy those improvements."[40] So the truth is out, we are not so selfless after all, and we really never have been. The pathetic thing is that so many Americans cannot accept selfish motivation in political affairs. But the rest of the world is tired of our pious pronouncements as if we were a self-sacrificing messiah nation.

Incidentally, the Meeting of Friends in Philadelphia took the President to task for his "distortion" of the Quaker position. While recognizing that Mr. Nixon has to be President for the entire people, and with no expectation that he would implement the Quaker views on war, nevertheless they protested the identification of his actions with the historic position of the Friends. They resented his wrapping himself in such religious association. They held that the policies in Vietnam do not square with the history of Quakers.[41]

The religion of Richard Nixon is simplistic and concentrated upon nineteenth-century virtues. For him faith demands that all action be useful, even recreation. The Puritan drive to justify even leisure as productive has found a real champion in President Nixon. One critic has described the Nixon volume *Six Crises* as a work written to display a "moral education." Morality is not very complex for the President, and the subtle distinctions of the "New Morality" would likely mean little to him. For Mr. Nixon, youth should be "clean-cut," as should all moral decisions. It may be unfair to say that he has always "looked on religion through Cecil B. De Mille's eyes,"[42] but Nixon does view decisions in terms of the "right-wrong" mentality. To be sure, he recognizes the gray areas of policy making, but he seems dominated by the thought that there is *a* "right way to do a thing." Right is defined for him through traditional Puritan moralisms for both domestic and foreign affairs.

The "Messianism" about which we have been speaking has been buttressed in recent years through a new kind of religious exercise. Reinhold Niebuhr described it as "The King's Chapel." Shortly after entering the White House Mr. Nixon set up a "by invitation only" religious service there for his administrative family. This antiseptic service functioned well to establish at long last what has lingered on the fringes for so many years—a genuine and defined civil religion. Probably it would horrify Professor Bellah. Niebuhr said: "he has established a conforming religion by semiofficially inviting representatives of all the disestablished religions . . ."[43] Michael Novak has pointed out that these services are the product of interest-group religion with none of the common people present. Billy Graham told Mrs. Lyndon Johnson that the services would allow the President to invite people to the White House who otherwise might not come. Interestingly, most all of them endorse the Nixon line in prayer and proclamation.

The "established religion" which Mr. Nixon sponsors was

designed, he said, to further the cause of religion. Apart from the serious question of this being a flagrant violation of the First Amendment, the nature of this establishment lends itself to support administrative policies. Those invited to declaim on the White House pulpit stage have regularly been unwilling to speak a word of judgment on political policy. It would be bad manners. Of course one could refuse an invitation, but the number of refusals publicly announced has not been excessive. "Established religion, with or without legal sanction, is always chary of criticism, especially if it is relevant to public policy."[44]

Billy Graham, in Niebuhr's words, "a domesticated and tailored leftover from the wild and woolly frontier evangelistic campaigns," has been intimately involved in the effort to marry the sectarian faith to the will of the state. The Nixon-Graham doctrine has assumed that all religion is virtuous and, in addition, has sought to inspire in the public that type of religion which sees all public policy as virtuous. One hardly need be reminded of the alliance between priest and king in ancient Israel.

Mr. Nixon has a long and interesting association with clerics of many traditions, including Father John Cronin, a speech writer for him in the fifties. In all those relationships there has been little indication of clerical influence. Mr. Nixon, we suggest, does not change—only circumstances.

It is our task to perfect, to improve, to alter when necessary, but in all cases to go forward.

—FRANKLIN ROOSEVELT

VI • *Religion and the Domestic Scene*

For various reasons the presidential role in foreign affairs seems regularly to have claimed the major headlines since World War I. This sudden thrusting of a nation into international concerns was only one more indication of a changed world of the twentieth century. The world had altered little since the beginnings of civilization compared to the rapid change after the War. And, for better or worse, America was affected even in her isolationism after 1920. These facts may tend to hide the terrific revolution on the domestic front that was every bit as dramatic as the encounters with Fascists and Communists abroad. But because domestic policy is so much less dominated by ideology and is affected far more by public attitudes and sentiments of a personal nature, the lines of religious influence upon presidential policy decisions in this area are problematic.

In the day-to-day affairs of the government a modern President is far more limited than the population generally recognizes. The bureaucracy has grown to such magnitude that the President is partially a captive of the office. While he sets a moral tone and implements his ideas on the international level, he is far more restricted on the domestic scene. "The

President's political necessities take priority over ventures in social justice."[1] Thus, while no effort will be made to identify actions with ideology in any absolute way, we will attempt to delineate the most significant developments in the area of social justice since the presidency of Woodrow Wilson.

There seems to be general agreement among most observers that the high point of Wilson's first term was the passage in 1913 of the Federal Reserve Act. Two other laws of note during the first year of his administration were the establishment of the Federal Trade Commission and the Clayton Anti-Trust Act. The latter was described by Samuel Gompers as the "charter of freedom for labor," excluding, as it did, the unions from prosecution under the act. It also recognized the right to picket and to boycott. Samuel Morison believes Wilson converted the Democratic Party from a states rights tradition to "enlightened nationalism."[2] Wilson spoke plainly against greed and class discrimination.

Before his second term could well begin, the World War was upon the nation and domestic matters were sidetracked for most of the rest of the Wilson years. While his ill-fated train tour to save the League ended in abject failure and physical collapse, his presidency has, until the present, inspired men of vastly different qualities. For instance, he is now in Richard Nixon's pantheon, and he is also a source of idealism for the former editor of the *Saturday Review,* Norman Cousins.[3]

President Wilson's quality of mind and spirit were evident in his remarkable collage of addresses. His New Freedom concept caught the imagination of idealists, ideologues, and realists alike. In domestic affairs his religion was the source of social action. This, however, did not prevent blindness on race. Whatever progress had been made in race relations before 1913 was abruptly halted under Wilson, and only after 1932 did a President seek to apply the Constitution to all citizens. During Wilson's administration civil servants were rigidly segregated according to race, and there were numerous dismissals from public office predicated upon racial bigotry.

Wilson's Christian faith was the driving force of his life. No one in the history of the White House could equal his mastery of the Bible, nor could anyone surpass his knowledge of theology. His religion supplied a certain vision, though restricted, that guided him in seeking justice. His "virtue," so troublesome in foreign affairs, set the stage for the social revolution of the thirties. And this is an interesting point. When men of Calvinistic tradition begin to speak of social justice they often come alive and shake off the shackles of dogmatism. This is only possible when they are not wedded to an economic system which precludes state action to alleviate suffering and poverty.

The most productive event of the Harding presidency was the Naval Conference on disarmament. Harding had no appreciable impact on the domestic scene. The end of his career was clouded with scandal. Business was allowed to extend itself without restriction and the twenties became a time of general social unconcern on the part of government. The death of Walter Rauschenbusch signaled the close of the first phase of the Social Gospel. That which first replaced it and took its name was an unreal utopianism that presumed automatic progress. This provided for the "second coming" of the Gospel of Wealth with its lack of concern for the poor and deprived. The twenties fostered a most corrupt time in our history, while "righteous" politicians and churchmen felt smug under legal prohibition of alcoholic beverages. The resulting crime and deterioration of morals pointed to the impossibility of legalizing morality conceived on the basis of an ancient code. The law must properly concern itself with justice, equality, and freedom, but legalized social mores seldom contribute to the health of the society. President Harding provided absolutely no moral leadership through his office, introducing a degree of laxity in simple decency in the White House that was distressing. Harding was, by objective standards unfit for the responsibilities of President.

The career of Calvin Coolidge marked the development in full flower of the Gospel of Wealth. Coolidge suppled a modicum of stability in the presidential office and revived decency in the White House after the onerous Harding days. In some remarkable way, perhaps because the majority of citizens did not really care, Coolidge overcame the blighting effect of moral desuetude and won election in 1924.

Coolidge was a perfect mirror of the times. No more than had his predecessor did he concern himself with matters of social justice. His ethics supported the success motif of business with a policy of inaction. Oddly, the number of memorable events during his years makes one wonder how he kept so "cool." During his presidency William Jennings Bryan died for his faith, fighting for biblical irrelevancy in a little Tennessee town. The year 1925 marked the founding of the American Civil Liberties Union. Coolidge presided over a nation that sent Charles Lindbergh over the Atlantic and Babe Ruth over home plate sixty times in 1927. He left the White House within a month of the St. Valentine's Day Massacre in Chicago. Massive social change due to the automobile, the airplane, and radio permanently affected the course of history. However, "since the President exalted inactivity to a fine art, there is not much to say about his administration . . ."[4]

President Hoover did in fact return "moral leadership" to the White House but the Depression robbed him of a worthy image and deprived him of the opportunity to lead. His Calvinistic convictions concerning the economics of collectivism, and his commitment to the Protestant ethic of reward for work, immobilized him in the face of the 1929 disaster and later turned him into a bitter man. He lived for more than thirty years as one whose name was synonymous with Depression while the nation he loved experienced unmatched prosperity. He resented his role in the drama. He was a good man, always

concerned for oppressed and needy people. His failure to recognize the character of social sin, his too easy reliance upon
self-help, prevented his humanitarianism from becoming positively active.

On the problem of alcohol Hoover was criticized from
both sides. He saw the signs of the times while in office and
knew the end was in sight for the Eighteenth Amendment. The
drys sensed this and were angry. On the other hand, Hoover
made every effort to effectively enforce the law. This angered
the wets.

Hoover did not take positive steps to alleviate the plight of
the Negro. W. E. B. Du Bois said that Hoover made "fewer
first-class appointments of Negroes to office than any President
since Andrew Jackson."[5] Hoover's Christian caring seemingly
was incapable of mobilizing government forces because his
Christian theology told him it would only harm the character
of the people. As a man he gave integrity to the office of President, but lacked ability to grapple satisfactorily with specific
issues.

> No quarter-century of American history had wrought so many
> changes in society, or so few in politics. . . . After a century and
> a half of asking the world to "give me your tired, your poor, your
> huddled masses yearning to breathe free," her door was shut.
> . . . After three centuries in which Christian morals had been
> maintained by law, religion, and custom, "permissiveness" had
> conquered St. Augustine and John Milton, becoming a dominant
> principle in education and sexual relations.[6]

In this way did Samuel Morison contrast the reactionary nature
of government with the social upheaval of the times.

Franklin Roosevelt brought a realism to the office of President which encouraged hope of recovery from the Depression.
In many ways FDR the man was never as admired as was
Herbert Hoover. Certainly the public had more lingering questions about FDR's "morals" than they ever had about the

THE CASH-REGISTER CHORUS

Fitzpatrick in the St. Louis *Post-Dispatch*   Used by permission.

CARRY ON!

Doyle in the Philadelphia "Record"

humanitarian Quaker. Roosevelt, however, acted to overcome the economic collapse of the nation and thereby served millions in need. Driven by a concern for persons in distress, the wealthy New Yorker turned the economic corner in America and introduced the welfare state. For this he was despised by Republicans and castigated by many of "his kind of people." Under his able administration the country not only recovered from the Depression, it also began the Social Security program which brought a fine sense of self-respect and dignity to millions of laboring men and women. The speeches of Roosevelt reflect his concern for equality of opportunity between the sexes. He was the first President consistently to employ the phrase "men and women."

Today, Roosevelt's concern in race relations might seem tame, but for his own day the movements he inaugurated were earth-shaking. Eleanor Roosevelt may have outdistanced her husband in speaking for human rights, angering her patrician associates in the process. As a moral leader in the nation, Mrs. Roosevelt stands alone among wives of Presidents. It was FDR who named the first Negro to the federal bench, and after more than two-thirds of a century of Republican loyalty, he took the Black vote for the Democrats. In 1936 the NAACP endorsed Roosevelt and broke with the party of Lincoln. In a wider area of human relations, FDR cracked religious and ethnic taboos. Of the 214 federal judges appointed from Harding through Hoover, eight had been Catholic and eight Jewish. Of the 196 Roosevelt appointments, fifty-one were Catholic and eight Jewish.[7] In the late thirties FDR was confronted with several Supreme Court vacancies which he filled with men of quality— Stone, Frankfurter, Black, Douglas, Jackson.

During his long term in office the churches began an upsurge in theology which came to flower in "Neoorthodoxy" under the brilliant leadership of Reinhold Niebuhr and Paul Tillich. By 1940 Niebuhr had become an enthusiastic Roosevelt

Democrat. The interplay between FDR's "brain trust" and Niebuhr is best documented in the statement of George Kennan, who said Niebuhr was "father to us all." His realism tempered with the ethic of Jesus undercut the Gospel of Wealth and established the standard of social justice for theologians of the forties and fifties. He became the theologian of the New Deal.

Roosevelt's sense of justice had many roots. His associates as well as his wife attributed this sensitivity to a deep faith, always a private faith. The frequent usage of prayer and the Bible in his addresses was more than political sagacity. For FDR the quest for social justice was hard and difficult work which he gladly accepted. In the miserable days of the thirties it is likely that Roosevelt's domestic realism coupled with devotion to freedom and justice avoided any serious challenge to our economic order by Communism. It was not ideological rejection of a system, but fervent acceptance of justice that proved most effective.

The death of Roosevelt and the consequent period of adjustment for President Truman affected the domestic scene for many months. In any case the War had engaged the nation beyond much thought for "home" issues. However, within a year Mr. Truman had to cope with the problem of dismantling a war machine without creating a disastrous recession. The post-war years brought wholly unexpected changes to the domestic arena, startling and often confusing the American public. A diverse America came hard up against the myth of the "melting pot" and found it wanting. There were multitudes of disadvantaged, poor and illiterate, in the nation, and their needs were not realized in the "American Dream." The issues of race, urbanization, economics, and suburbia vied for major attention as the fifties approached. A predicted high rise in population caused dismay among educators who could not convince the public of pending difficulties. The problem of the elderly was compounded by the advances in medical science, prompting Harry Truman to propose medical aid for the aged. It seemed that most of the citizens were mesmerized during evening hours by watching television in their living rooms. Truman, who entered the White House to the roar of atomic energy and left to the carping of Joe McCarthy, presided over the most momentous decade in our history, what Eric Goldman has described as "The Crucial Decade." The record shows that President Truman provided domestic stability.

It was in the area of race that President Truman distinguished himself. It was Truman who created the Commission on Civil Rights; it was he who sought to establish a Fair Employment Practices Commission; it was he who fought the Senate filibuster. His native liberalism, born of his sense of fairness, produced sterling results in the field of social justice. He seemed to come by his sentiments through religious belief as well as by the example of his predecessor.

The question of the domestic influence of Communism had become serious for the President by 1951. As we have noted, he crusaded with vigor in fighting Communism abroad, but his record at home does not reflect any attempt to alarm the nation at the expense of civil liberties. He had faith in his country, an innate feeling of the rightness of the American way, which would not allow him to tamper with the fundamental documents of our history, particularly the Bill of Rights. It was the very absence of a civil religion dogma that protected the rights of the minority. The internal hostility sapped the strength of many, but the President stood solidly against the onslaught of the witch-hunters. Truman saw no reason to fear "upset from within." In his *Memoirs* he wrote: "If we cannot have confidence in our neighbors and the teachers who are teaching our children, then our country is in trouble."[8]

The election of Dwight Eisenhower in 1952 over the well-qualified and exceptionally gifted Adlai Stevenson was inevita-

"I Think This Is Rather A Sad Sort Of Thing . . ."

From *Straight Herblock* (Simon & Schuster, 1964)

ble. Korea and Harry Vaughan and twenty years of the Democrats had made it so. It mattered not at all that Stevenson
offered credentials far superior to his opponent. His government service after 1956 demonstrated his broad vision and keen
insights. Stevenson was a Jeffersonian with just the touch of
realism that made him an ideal candidate at precisely the wrong
time in history. Unitarian in background, he was extremely
conscious of the worth of man and human dignity. Like Jefferson, his faith in justice and freedom was a political credo. But,
like Roosevelt, he controlled his vision with realistic rationality.
His humor cracked the stolid fifties with a political wit for a
generation that would not laugh. The times called for an Eisenhower, as they had in another day demanded a Harding.

Eisenhower was a timid President, believing in states'
rights to such a degree that it took three years to do anything
toward implementing the 1954 Supreme Court decision on discrimination in the schools. He moved then into Little Rock
only because his presidential authority had been challenged. In
the most effective act of his presidency, he had appointed Earl
Warren as Chief Justice of the Supreme Court. But having done
that, he made little effort through administrative action to support the Court's findings. While he talked incessantly about the
need for voluntary acceptance of the Negro as a member of the
social order, he refused federal interference to that end. His
"view of civil rights for the Negro was . . . paternalistic, straight
out of the nineteenth century."[9] His overwhelming popularity
in the South in 1956 attests to his being "safe" on race.

Unlike Truman, Eisenhower capitulated to the McCarthy-
McCarren combine and rooted out "security risks" in govern-
ment, always in a genteel fashion. Eisenhower sacrificed his
Secretary of the Army to the vicious pummeling of Senator
McCarthy and left the nation to be rescued by a little known
New England lawyer, Joseph Welch. Eisenhower was the most
pious of Presidents though he provided little moral leadership
for the nation in distress.

In civil rights legislation Eisenhower trod lightly, though his administration "witnessed the passage of the first civil rights laws since the post–Civil War era. The Eisenhower administration exhibited at least a limited recognition that the general disposition of the Coolidge-Harding-Hoover era opposing federal assertion in behalf of the disadvantaged had become obsolete in the practice of the Presidency. It alienates too many voters."[10]

The years of Kennedy, Johnson, and Nixon have been chaotic domestically. Not only did they bring a rash of assassinations and terrific unrest in the ghetto areas of the cities, but the very nature of the educational system has been tested by student protests. Striving for social justice has been increasingly resisted by the "silent majority," and frantic protests over a bloody and senseless war have availed little. Rexford G. Tugwell observed that in recent years the President has found the entire domestic policy area more and more complicated by many congressmen who "never have to put forward any project for the good of the country if it happens not to be good for them."[11] It will be some time before events are in sufficient perspective to pass historical judgment. It is too early to appraise pressures on the President with respect to domestic issues; so we have attempted only a brief survey of the most critical internal problems that confront the nation.

John Kennedy came to the White House with a concern about two serious matters—education and the minimum wage. He soon discovered that Congress was not moved by his campaign oratory on these matters. JFK had assumed that he could by "vigorous use of power and personality . . . overcome all obstacles and move the country."[12] Congress taught him otherwise. At his death his domestic policies were stalled in the halls of the legislature and many despaired of their passage.

The ugly mood of the late sixties was just manifesting itself as JFK came to office. He identified with the cause of Martin Luther King, who in the fifties had valiantly worked and risked for constitutional freedom. Kennedy's chief worry here was the establishment of justice for all alike. Legislation to that end had to wait until after his death.

Kennedy was moved by a moral sense for the rights of man. He listened to youth and respected the young, so he established the Peace Corps which enlisted young men and women to do battle against ignorance and disease in all parts of the world. The plan had a freshness about it that appealed to both idealists and realists. Kennedy was in the process of restoring a genuine national pride when the vision ended in Dallas. That death coupled with that of his brother and King has unleashed a veritable whirlwind of sentiments which, when joined with the revulsion at the war in Vietnam, are yet undetermined in their final effects.

Lyndon Johnson forced the Kennedy program through a receptive Congress, and this series of legislation became a monument to him as well as to his predecessor. LBJ came to believe with all his being in the kind of freedom anticipated in the 1964 Civil Rights Act. Once when Johnson had gathered prominent businessmen to discuss that Act, he told them about their Negro cook who rode in the automobile with him and "Bird" back and forth to Texas. He explained that when they stopped he had to find a special bathroom for their friend. He asked the men if this was America. He was appealing to them to get in behind the Act and support it. His fervor and his "tremendously mobile face" made him a strong advocate for his position.

When LBJ was asked how he explained his shift on voting rights, something he had opposed in the Senate, he gave two sound reasons. First, he was no longer Senator from Texas, representing those people. He was President of all the people. Second, he declared that we all learn.

Johnson had a sense of awe about the office of President. No man, it has been observed, has been more affected by the position itself.[13] In Johnson's opinion the President is steward of all of the people from whom he has a moral charge. This charge has been intensified by the possibility of nuclear war, by the heaping of power in the office of President, and by the diversity within the nation itself—the President is the only symbol of *all* the people. In fact, that is why the President can, in foreign affairs, more easily impose his values on that office. Strong personalities have shaped the position to their images. "In foreign affairs presidents can make the most momentous commitments and not be seriously opposed unless the adventures prove disastrous . . ."[14]

Johnson's "Great Society" and "War on Poverty" were overshadowed by the magnitude of the expanding conflict in Southeast Asia. It seems as if his idealistic programs were swallowed in the ideology that escalated the war in Vietnam. We are yet too close to pass final judgment.

Richard Nixon is still in the process of spelling out his domestic program. Most of his efforts have reflected caution. His view of the Supreme Court has undoubtedly created far-reaching effects for the future. His general conservatism on matters of racial justice, especially implementation, may yet cause a severe clash between the Supreme Court and the Chief Executive. The President's appointments to high office have disturbed those who cherish the Bill of Rights, particularly his assignment of John Mitchell to the office of Attorney General. He is hardly in the tradition of his immediate predecessors. The still unsettling specter of Vice-President Spiro Agnew does not give encouragement to those who love freedom. Further, Agnew should be a permanent reminder to both parties to take the selection of the second position on the ticket seriously. But Nixon is in midstream. Hard judgments as to his activities in the domestic sphere would be too journalistic for statement here. The concluding chapter will deal with speculative analysis.

The time has come for us as a people, as a community learning together, to learn how to assume conscious control of our destiny.

—ADLAI STEVENSON

VII • *Beyond Messianism*

1 • THE PRESIDENCY AND MESSIANISM

The early Presidents were men of little formal religious persuasion. They saw religion as a private affair. Thomas Jefferson gave expression to religious impulses when he became engaged politically. Religion for him was life, reason, politics. He was an idealist dreaming more than reality could offer. Deism was a part of his politics. In the language of modern ethics, he had a "goal morality," intending to establish justice in the land. Jefferson championed what Paul Tillich called the "holiness of what ought to be." His liberalism looked forever forward. Lincoln was the last President who held that idea about religion. Many have claimed to be disciples of Jefferson but few were truly oriented toward the future. Most disproved their discipleship by looking back.

Men like Woodrow Wilson, uneasy with conflict between the way things are and the way things ought to be, are convinced of the need to moralize about the wide chasm between their private religious faith and the current circumstances.

Looking back to ancient religious and political revelations they became ideologists, seeking to force the present into agreement with God's law, long revealed. It is "special revelation" that makes them look to the past rather than forward. These legalistic moralists gave us visions like the League of Nations, yet they inspired an American "Messianism" which binds the United States policy to some previous interpretation of the law of God. For them "democracy alone is regarded as the Christian form of the state."[1]

Then there have been the religious realists, the Anglicans among us, of whatever formal religious affiliation. Roosevelt and Kennedy made their way between the Jeffersonian goals and the Wilsonian laws to a realistic appraisal of circumstances as they arose. They were "situation" ethicists. Like the moralists and the idealists, these pragmatists had limitations as to both vision and achievement. They tended toward gullibility in personal diplomacy and often depended too much upon their "charisma," a product of their pragmatism. It seems likely that a modified political realist will be most effective in directing United States policy for the future. By "modified" we suggest that the realism must be tempered by the morality of the idealist with proper appreciation for, and understanding of, *demythologized* history. Then, and only then, will "Messianism" pass from our midst. Louis Hartz has described this idealist-realist combination well.

> When liberty does not exist in a society even though the history of that society has been different from the history of any we may be familiar with, I say that society is open to criticism because liberty is not present in it. On the other hand, and here we come down to what seems to be the root of the matter, what we have to do is disentangle our faith in the norm of freedom from the peculiar historic experience in which it has been cast in the United States. We have to be able to distinguish the universality of an ethic from the peculiar framework in which we have received it.[2]

GETTING TOGETHER!
Cassel in the New York *Evening World*

2 • CIVIL RELIGION ONCE AGAIN

Emil Durkheim, in analyzing primitive society, has drawn interesting and impressive conclusions concerning religion. His work has received attention by many leading theologians as well as sociologists. For him society was the source of religion. Does this mean that the explanation for all religion lies in society? Even though civil religion was a necessary product of primitive society, can modern society be said to have progressed beyond that? A too ready acceptance of Durkheim's results for all society issues in sociological determinism. But the man who has radically restructured his environment and the scientist who is never mastered by the past make this kind of determinism look foolish. There is no reasonable explanation of America on the basis of Australian aboriginals, unless we blindly accept the "It is written" mentality. An excellent challenge to the thesis of social solidarity is offered by John F. Wilson. He feels we must overcome impulses in the direction of such solidarity as "a necessary precondition for modern man to construct the differentiated and pluralistic urban cultures which seem to offer the only hope for world humanity."[3]

For Durkheim any community that has beliefs and rites is perforce practicing religion. Society creates God and rational man will not continue to worship such a God. So Durkheim felt that "religion in the spiritual sense" was doomed, but he hoped for "a secular assembly, a secularist religion of a humanist kind."[4] He used the French Revolution and its emphasis upon liberty, equality, and fraternity to illustrate his expectations. He wrote: "There can be no society which does not feel the need of upholding and reaffirming at regular intervals the collective sentiments and the collective ideas which make its unity and its personality."[5] He insists there is "no essential difference" between Christian worship and "some great event in the national life." He concludes: "A society is the most powerful combination of physical and moral forces of which nature offers us an example."[6] Society is God. Individualism and transcendence are denied.

The problem with Durkheim is not merely his conclusions, but the assumptions that the conclusions are inevitable. The type of civil religion of which Durkheim is thinking is ably expounded in an essay by Conrad Cherry in which he delineates the dangers inherent in the rising religion of the state in America.[7]

Quite appropriately, Robert Bellah envisions the *best* in the Constitution and the Declaration of Independence as synonymous with the *best* in the civil religion. The problem is to define "best." Best for whom? The following assertion about the Declaration of Independence might be stoutly affirmed by a large number of citizens. "There is no question of contradiction between democracy and Christ . . . [there is] a relationship of enlarged and deepened affirmation as between the truths of the Declaration and the perspective of the mind of One who came as 'the way, the truth, and the life.'"[8] It is all very well for Bellah to insist that such affirmations are distortions of the "true" civil religion, but what data supports this position? Surely not only the basic documents of our history, but ceremonies, prayers, and rites as well are open to a variety of conflicting interpretations. The backers of "Messianism" claim Jefferson and Lincoln as strongly as do the political realists and idealists. There is no way to establish an American orthodox civil religion and at the same time maintain the freedom of the national liberal tradition.

An analogy with the church is instructive. By his understanding of God Jesus preached service, not salvation; yet through the centuries the church has seldom heeded the teachings of Jesus while it continually proclaimed soul salvation as its primary function. This emphasis has been enshrined in doctrine so completely that to challenge may lead to ostracism. Orthodoxy reduces Jesus and turns him from prophet into God. Ultimately this means that his words no longer matter since the church worships him. The only way to recover the freedom of Jesus is to set him free from dogma, not just bad dogma, but *all* dogma.

The historic religious traditions of Judaism and Christianity have never been far removed from willingness to join in with missionary nationalism. The sermons of the Calvinist Samuel Davies, champion of religious toleration in the colony of Virginia, were so laced with "God and country" that one admirer called him the "best recruiting officer in the colony" during the French and Indian War. From the Puritans in New England through Wilson to Nixon there is the confident faith in an absolute morality which America possesses. From the New Israel of Massachusetts to the Christian chauvinism of White House religious services, it is abundantly clear that any potential civil religion is not in need of "continual reformation" but of continual scrutiny by citizens of all faiths and of no faith. There does not now appear to be *a* civil religion but if one evolves it will surely bear the shape of all formal state religion —a creedal endorsement of the object of faith, in this case national policy. This would be true whether the policy be liberal or conservative.

The Puritan movement grew to maturity in America through an emphasis upon salvation. It was the clarion call of the Great Awakening with Jonathan Edwards and it has been the supreme pronouncement of the Christian leadership from Dwight L. Moody to Billy Graham. Because of the exclusiveness of salvation, grounded in a religion of revelation, it easily became transformed into extreme nationalism or "Messianism." If Jefferson and Lincoln succeeded to any degree in breaking the hold of that type of thinking, the mass of citizens has rarely shared the freedom. To the extent that we presently have in America *a* civil religion, it is a fruit of the salvation heritage.

The only means by which an establishment of that type can be voided is through reformation in the churches and by constant challenge to prevailing "Messianism" as a distortion of the Bill of Rights. The American people may be brought to appreciate their rich heritage only by the substitution of a liberal perspective for the prevailing drive for a civil religion.

There is evidence today that states are employing religion as a kind of glue or adhesive to bind the national will. States are often obvious in their usage of religious motifs, usually offensive to Americans. Yet, what of our own ceremonies and rites when baptized into a civil religion: are they too offensive? Many of our ceremonies are sanctified with prayer in the name of God who is the messianic God, not the prophetic God. In order to hold the majority to this God, he is identified with the Judeo-Christian God, and the church and the synagogue gladly contribute him. Only as the religious communities return to the spirit of the prophets will things change. Then the state will have to seek rational justification for its policies, instead of retreating into pious preachments.

A revitalized religious community oriented to the future would motivate the political community to behave in a manner that desires assessment in terms of deeds of justice rather than in terms of rites and ceremonies. This future orientation is not the futurism of salvation religion, but realistic, this-world centered. The good in the American tradition does not require mythologizing in order to be appreciated. When God is injected as the prime mover, the progressive thinking of the founding fathers is translated into the "great tradition." That change ignores the significant fact that those very figures whom we regard with reverence had no such rites and rituals. They faced reality with an open, free mind and a free spirit. Attitude can be learned from the past, spirit can be felt, but any establishment of national dogma, religious or political, only imposes enslavement on little minds.

3 • THE BILL OF RIGHTS

In recent discussions of civil religion little attention has been devoted to the Bill of Rights. I suppose that the first ten amendments would be one of the documents in any American civil religion, although there are indications that the ideas set forth in these articles are obnoxious to a majority of present-day citizens. Indeed, we need to remember that those amendments were added to protect the majority from itself as well as the minority from the tendency toward totalitarianism. Judicial review secured these guarantees. To be sure, if a society really wanted to deny freedom to the minority, or to itself for that matter, it would only be a question of time before the goal was accomplished. The Bill of Rights, is, at best, a restraint. The nation's founders did not deem it wise, however, merely to admonish future legislatures not to impair basic freedoms as violation of human rights. They affirmed these freedoms in constitutional form.

In the broad definition of the term, Jefferson's phrase about the wall between church and state has become a proof text for the First Amendment. But it means a great deal more. Neither Jefferson, nor anyone else, intended to separate religion from government when religion was construed as an individual faith. And, in fact, private devotion did affect the national weal from the beginning. The present emphasis upon civil religion is, however, a flagrant toying with the First Amendment.

Unfortunately, separation of church and state became for many Americans a prime doctrine which was manipulated into support of bigotry, racism, and anti-Catholicism. The phrase now has a bad name among progressives. Yet, the principle of religious liberty is the real key. Up to the present the Supreme Court has been able to maintain the legal concept. Various

trends in the national life suggest that a civil religion of the
majority might find religious liberty something it did not care
to preserve. Senator Everett Dirksen gave the nation fair warning on that.

4 • THE FUTURE

How are we able to make sense out of national ceremonies without seeing them in religious dimension? Ceremonies are of value to the psychological health of the population.
The danger arises when documents of the ceremonies become
"scripture" thus enforceable against the consciences of many
citizens. The "love it or leave it" mentality may predominate.
The state, after all, is not comparable to the church. There is
no voluntary principle of association operative in a political
state.

Civil religion with "scripture" tends to deify the state.
Every man with political ambition who rises to high office is
prone to interpret his own actions as the fulfillment of the
"true" civil religion and as such above criticism. President
Johnson did that in the fall of 1967 when he stumped the
country on behalf of his Vietnam policy. President Nixon does
that when he appears on television to tell the "truth" to the
people because, so he says, citizens have been misled by journalists, educators, politicians, and assorted other persons. Any
civil religion would become a powerful instrument of the state,
identified with the ruler and his own personal view of the
American past. Like a god, the President could manipulate the
religion to suit his intentions. The threat of this national cult
should cause the Judeo-Christian communities to reexamine

their role in the government. As prophetic faiths, at their best, they have found a norm and standard *beyond* the civil society. A national cult will only direct the public in pride to self-worship.

It is unrealistic to presume that a liberal interpretation of Lincoln and Kennedy can be parlayed into a national religion. Society's cult will be the lowest common denominator. National cults will avoid sharp edges just as astute politicians avoid them. A wily public servant will not soon miss the measure of success to be gained from being "God's man." Senator Dirksen knew that an election year was no time to vote against prayer as he struggled to amend the Bill of Rights to establish a religion. Politics needs humanization, not deification. That can be done best not by reforming the politician's state religion, but by reforming American Christianity and Judaism.

John Kennedy was often concerned about the degree to which our historic myths have tied our hands in dealing with the present. And there has been no President in our nearly two hundred years with a greater appreciation of history. It is devastating irony that he has become the most mythologized of Presidents. This procedure glosses over the man.[9]

Bellah insists that "the American civil religion is not the worship of the American nation but an understanding of the American experience in the light of ultimate and universal reality."[10] However, he is here describing the genius of the American experience in historical perspective, not a religion. If we ever reduce it to a ceremonialized religion it will be the poorer. A real and dynamic state cult *would* eventuate in "worship of the American nation." Bellah does admit that this so-called religion "has not always been invoked in favor of worthy causes."[11] It is just at this point that the issue is clearly drawn. What causes *are* worthy? Who decides? Should any nation embark on causes? Woodrow Wilson failed, in some degree, because he dedicated himself to a holy "cause." President Johnson had a "cause" in Vietnam which played havoc with the nation. Richard Nixon has a "cause" to restore morality, law, order, and decency to the United States, to reassert the economic success motif in American life. Religious cults are invoked to support the "cause." Has not our basic malaise since 1917 in international relations been partially a result of the anti-Communist "cause"? "Anyone at the battle line realizes it would be immoral to go around killing men for a Cause."[12]

In his stunning book *Nixon Agonistes* Garry Wills discusses the American tradition, politically, as identical with "abject devotion to success."[13] He describes the Horatio Alger success stories as synonymous with the "American Way of Life." Chief advocates of that form were Christian ministers who insisted that economic advancement was a sure sign of divine reward. Russell Conwell epitomized this American cult, the secular religion of success. The Presidents of this century have yet to rid themselves of this baggage which appears in the conduct of foreign as well as domestic affairs.

Wills makes this assessment of Nixon respecting his devotion to causes. "No wonder Nixon feels an affinity for Wilson. Believers in the self-made man at home, both dealt in the 'self-determined' nations abroad, and gave an evangelical flavor to their exhortations for an 'open world' of peaceful competition between such nations."[14] Continuing, Wills writes plainly:

> The attempt to be nationally "selfless" is not only confused and confusing, but wrong. The state should not take any position toward other states except from "reasons of state." It is immoral —not reasonable—for the state to act as something other than what it is. Presidents are not elected, as Wilson thought he was, to create a new world in the American image, but to administer the country's resources in the country's interest.[15]

If self-interest self-consciously enlightened by a grasp of the heritage of the past directed our international policy, the nation could shed its miasma of "Messianism." The progressive should abandon civil religion as an ideal, for even the best of it ends only in enlightened orthodoxy.

America has an abundance of myths that clutter and impede progress. Presidents do not need to mythologize their predecessors. Certainly myth has a place in the life and spirit of even a modern state. The flag is a myth, likewise Washington and Lincoln—myths in the sense that they evoke emotional response and a sense of common unity among the people, particularly in times of crisis. It would be pointless to tell the average American what he really means when he participates in ceremonies, e.g., saluting the flag. If, however, you make an issue of it, what he understands may be a long way from what you think it is. American leadership must find ways to capture with imagination that sense of national oneness through reasoned campaigns for justice in the social order. If they make this concept ring true, then one day the people may see that they have created a new, better, richer American mythology.

A sense of justice denuded of the political claptrap may be the finest expression of the continuing American experience.

The best in ourselves is not in our democratic institutions, or dedication to them. That kind of thinking ultimately spells death for the institution. The best in us is human values that have been encouraged in the system. American youth do not give credence to the argument for institutions as things to be revered. We surely should have learned this by now. What is required in us is a recognition that they are right. Then, maybe, if we could demonstrate the catalytic effect of democracy, we would be heard.

What do starving and poverty-stricken people care about free election? Elections have become a fetish. We may not take them seriously and by neglect sell our birthright to mediocrity in public office, but Americans are ready to fight to force everyone else to vote. This has not only affected progress within the nation but also clouded our international policy. We might be better advised to concern ourselves with people and their needs. The genius of our tradition is the belief that we do not need to dominate anyone. Why then should we try "for their own good" to become messianic about democracy in the world? Far better if we would use our freedom to communicate with others across ideological barriers. By that course we may demonstrate the power and vitality of freedom. Democracy ceases to exist when it becomes dogma. Our politics, foreign and domestic, need to recover that insight as we approach the two hundredth anniversary of the founding of this free nation.

5 • CONCLUSION

America needs an understanding of its role in world affairs. It has assumed, since the early days of the Republic, that it had something worth sharing with other peoples. This certainly was and is a fact. How is one to share? If the sharing becomes imposition or self-righteousness we may anticipate negative world response. There is something uncanny about the modern missionary movement receiving its impetus in England in 1792, during the first term of George Washington. The effect of that movement, which quickly spread to America, was to establish the foundations for huge modern denominational establishments and to provide an ideological basis for imperialism and colonialism in the West. The missionary-imperialist complex carried the Western culture to the "heathen" in other lands in the name of God. The economic advantage was terrific. Religion was often used as the "opiate of the people." The result was an assumption in the West of divine right and justice for all our causes. The missionary movement was often merely an extension of cultural imperialism. In a comment on this phase of the church's life, Eric Goldman noted:

> For many decades a feeling had been growing in America that the Asians were the special mission of the United States under the law of history. It was the American duty to help feed them, educate them, convert them, nudge them along toward the middle-class life.[16]

The connection between the Christian mission fervor and the "Messianism" of many Presidents has become of more particular importance in the present decade. The church itself has probably come to the close of the missionary phase of its history as defined by William Carey in 1792. Yet still from a thousand pulpits there can be heard on a weekly basis the words of ministers calling for sacrificial giving so that conversion may occur for some poor "unsaved" soul in "darkest" Africa or "heathen" India. This religious chauvinism blurs the line between God and country, thereby offering solace for those who dream of Christianizing and democratizing the world. In Southeast Asia Professor Brinton has noted the relation of these two forces. "I think as long as we attempt to either make available to or force the Western values on Vietnam of a pro-Western Christian-led democracy, the war may last a long time."[17]

President Richard Nixon is still seemingly locked in this ideological jungle, struggle as he may to sound new and progressive. He continues the Christian dream of American destiny. The missionary thrust of American foreign policy is characterized by assertion of unmatched military might, total technological supremacy, and invincible benevolence.

The problem is an involved one. Jefferson believed we had something worthwhile and valuable for all people. How does one go about sharing possessions? Clearly not by missionary zeal and conversion. "It is when America is in her most altruistic mood that other nations better get behind their bunkers."[18]

We have to take a realistic look, not a sentimental one, at our history. We shall have to admit that most international conflicts have been for national self-interest. As long as we continue to insist as a nation that we are misunderstood and really mean only to help others, never ourselves, the nations of the world will wonder. We should admit that the natural resources of Southeast Asia are an important part of our national security as construed by the White House. This does not imply that our motives for entering Vietnam were evil. It is to recognize that they were far from altruistic and may have been ill-advised. Ted Sorenson said the most vexing problem for President Kennedy in his last days was Vietnam. An issue that complex cannot legitimately be simplified by moralizing.

For the future, the United States is going to have to admit its own genuine interests in dealing with the world community. Our security as a nation was involved in the Second World War. As long as a majority of the American people are satisfied that national interest is involved, foreign policy is secure. When that interest can no longer sustain an action, leaders roll out the destiny argument. What is needed is foreign policy that does not need to be "sold" to the public, but carries its own credentials. In a democracy secrecy will always lead to trouble.

If America is to reach maturity, religious leadership will have to mature. With the recent loss of Reinhold Niebuhr the nation does not have a cogent voice to whom it will listen. The traditional religious patterns affecting political life are moribund and anachronistic. Our investigation has shown that in most instances religion influenced the Presidents chiefly in childhood. Whereas these men grew in all other ways, their religion remained static. The church had no voice. All too often the President's minister reflected the kindly, out-of-touch image projected by Hollywood. By a process of compounded delays a modern President could be trapped with mid-nineteenth-century theology. If a President ended his religious training while still a boy, the schools that instructed his minister could well have been seeking to preserve some pre–Civil War orthodoxy.

The United States does not require any more thundering messages on free elections abroad. It needs men and women who will soberly heed all reasonable voices and then act in the best interest of the nation. If the United States has virtue in its character and heritage, then such an approach will result in good for the world in which we are an unapologetically interested party.

Perhaps in the spring of 1972 there will be a man like Kennedy or Stevenson or Lincoln to inspire the people, but the present prospects are not bright. "Whatever the explanation, lack of leadership is the most prominent feature on our political landscape, and lack of creativity the most striking characteristic of our political life."[19] The tragedy of this situation is that most observers do not think this nation can afford another political vacuum similar to the twenties. Conservatives and liberals alike need to talk in terms of vitality and rationality about the present if the two parties are to be made travel-worthy for the last third of the century. In 1960 Adlai Stevenson warned the nation that its "little aims and large fears" had in them the seed of destruction. The country can discover the presidential leadership it requires if it will cease elevating mediocrity and envision what Tillich calls the "holiness of what is." The wise man expertly blends and discreetly uses all his treasures, both new and old.

Notes

CHAPTER I

1. Robert N. Bellah, "Civil Religion in America," *Daedalus*, Vol. 96, No. 1 (Winter 1967), p. 1.
2. Though Bellah properly credits Rousseau as originator of the phrase, I believe his current use of it comes from reading Louis Hartz's *The Liberal Tradition in America*. Hartz projects a unitary concept of the American tradition quite consistent with Bellah. See page 39 of Hartz for reference to civil religion.
3. Martin Marty, *The New Shape of American Religion* (New York: Harper & Row, 1959), p. 69.
4. Press conference during the Southern Baptist Convention in May 1964. I was present at the conference and asked the questions.
5. Marty, *op. cit.,* p. 88.
6. Bellah, *op. cit.,* p. 19.
7. H. Richard Niebuhr, *The Social Sources of Denominationalism* (New York: Meridian Books, 1957), p. 264.
8. Sidney Verba, "The Kennedy Assassination and the Nature of Political Commitment," *The Kennedy Assassination and the American Public*, ed. Bradley S. Greenberg and Edwin B. Parker (Stanford, Calif.: Stanford University Press, 1965), p. 354.
9. Lewis Lipsitz, "If, as Verba Says, the State Functions as a Religion, What Are We to Do Then to Save Our Souls?," *The American Political Science Review*, Vol. 62, No. 2 (1968), p. 530.
10. John F. Wilson, "The Status of 'Civil Religion' in America," *The Religion of the Republic*, ed. Elwyn Smith (Philadelphia: Fortress Press, 1971), p. 10.
11. *Ibid.,* p. 12.

CHAPTER II

1. Suggested works include Winthrop Hudson, *The Great Tradition of the American Churches;* Evarts B. Greene, *Religion and the State;* Anson P. Stokes and Leo Pfeffer, *Church and State in the United States.*
2. See Winthrop Hudson, *The Great Tradition of the American Churches* (New York: Harper & Brothers, 1953), Ch. II.
3. Alexis de Tocqueville, *Democracy in America,* ed. Phillips Bradley (New York: Alfred A. Knopf, 1945), Vol. I, pp. 303–305.
4. Bellah, *op. cit.,* p. 14. If he read the same newspapers I see daily he might not be so confident.
5. *Nationalism and Religion in America,* ed. W. S. Hudson (New York: Harper & Row, 1970), p. 120.

6. Francis H. Heller, *Introduction to American Constitutional Law* (New York: Harper & Brothers, 1952), pp. 549–550.

7. J. Paul Williams, *What Americans Believe and How They Worship* (New York: Harper & Brothers, 1952), p. 371.

8. *Ibid.,* p. 367.

9. *Ibid.,* p. 371.

10. H. Richard Niebuhr, *The Kingdom of God in America* (New York: Harper & Brothers, 1937), p. 179.

11. *Ibid.,* p. 178.

12. Louis W. Koenig, *The Chief Executive* (New York: Harcourt, Brace & World, 1968), p. 305.

CHAPTER III

1. Louis Hartz, "The Nature of Revolution," *Hearings Before the Committee on Foreign Relations,* United States Senate, Ninetieth Congress, Second Session (February 26, 1968), p. 118.

2. *Ibid.*

3. *Ibid.,* p. 133.

4. *Selected Literary and Political Papers and Addresses of Woodrow Wilson,* Vol. II (New York: Grosset & Dunlap, 1927), p. 277.

5. Letters and papers of Woodrow Wilson to be found in the Woodrow Wilson Collection, Firestone Library, Princeton University.

6. Hartz, *op. cit.,* p. 111.

7. Sigmund Freud and William C. Bullitt, *Thomas Woodrow Wilson: A Psychological Study* (Boston: Houghton Mifflin Co., 1967).

8. Woodrow Wilson Collection, Princeton University.

9. Crane Brinton, "The Nature of Revolution," *Hearings Before the Committee on Foreign Relations,* United States Senate, Ninetieth Congress, Second Session (February 19, 1968), p. 43.

10. Samuel Eliot Morison, *The Oxford History of the American People* (New York: Oxford University Press, 1965), p. 883.

11. Wilson Collection in the Manuscript Division of the Library of Congress, Washington, D.C.

12. *Selected Literary and Political Papers and Addresses of Woodrow Wilson, op. cit.,* Vol. I, p. 54.

13. *Ibid.*

14. *Ibid.,* p. 183.

15. Arthur Link, *Wilson: The Road to the White House* (Princeton: Princeton University Press, 1956), p. 321.

16. Wilson, *op. cit.,* p. 344.

17. Arthur M. Schlesinger, Jr., *The Crisis of the Old Order* (Boston: Houghton Mifflin Co., 1957), p. 50.

18. Francis Russell, *The Shadow of Blooming Grove: Warren G. Harding in His Times* (New York: McGraw-Hill Book Co., 1968), p. 160.

19. *Ibid.,* pp. 168–169.

20. Frederick Lewis Allen, *Only Yesterday* (New York: Bantam Books, 1957), p. 131.

21. Donald R. McCoy, *Calvin Coolidge: The Quiet President* (New York: The Macmillan Co., 1967), p. 56.

22. *Ibid.,* p. 150.

23. William Allen White, *A Puritan in Babylon: The Story of Calvin Coolidge* (New York: The Macmillan Co., 1939), p. 14.
24. Calvin Coolidge, *Autobiography of Calvin Coolidge* (New York: Cosmopolitan Book Corp., 1929).
25. McCoy, *op. cit.*, p. 414.
26. Karl Schriftgiesser, *This Was Normalcy* (Boston: Little, Brown & Co., 1948), p. 165.
27. Herbert Hoover, *The Memoirs of Herbert Hoover: The Cabinet and the Presidency, 1920–1933* (New York: The Macmillan Co., 1952), p. 56.
28. Allen, *op. cit.*, p. 129.
29. One wonders at the possible unconscious influence upon Arthur Larson's *Eisenhower: The President Nobody Knew.*
30. Hudson, *Great Tradition,* p. 180.
31. *Ibid.,* p. 184.
32. Herbert Hoover, *Addresses upon the American Road, 1933–1938* (New York: Charles Scribner's Sons, 1938), p. 160.
33. E. Digby Baltzell, *The Protestant Establishment: Aristocracy and Caste in America* (New York: Vintage Books, 1966), p. 227.
34. Hoover, *American Road, 1933–1938,* p. 270.
35. Ray L. Wilbur and Arthur M. Hyde, *The Hoover Policies* (New York: Charles Scribner's Sons, 1937), p. 7.
36. Hoover, *American Road, 1933–1938,* p. 315.
37. Harrison E. Salisbury, "Diplomacy: The Indivisible Peace," *The Soviet Union: The Fifty Years,* ed. Harrison Salisbury (New York: Harcourt, Brace & World, 1967), p. 442.
38. George F. Kennan, *Russia and the West Under Lenin and Stalin* (Boston: Little, Brown & Co., 1961), p. 138.
39. Hoover, *Memoirs, 1920–1933,* p. 182.
40. Herbert Hoover, *Addresses upon the American Road, 1948–1950* (Stanford, Calif.: Stanford University Press, 1951), p. 66.
41. *Ibid.,* p. 67.
42. Hans Morgenthau, "Democratic Ideology," *Control or Fate in Economic Affairs* (New York: The Academy of Political Science, 1971), Vol. XXX, No. 3, p. 204.
43. Herbert Hoover, *The Memoirs of Herbert Hoover: The Great Depression, 1929–1941* (New York: The Macmillan Co., 1952), pp. 350–356.
44. Hoover, *American Road, 1948–1950,* p. 9.
45. *Ibid.,* p. 175.

CHAPTER IV

1. Samuel I. Rosenman, *Working with Roosevelt* (New York: Harper & Brothers, 1952), p. 24.
2. Walter Lippmann, *Interpretations, 1931–1932* (New York: The Macmillan Co., 1932), p. 273.
3. Louis Hartz, *The Liberal Tradition in America* (New York: Harcourt, Brace & World, 1955), p. 270.
4. Thomas H. Greer, *What Roosevelt Thought* (East Lansing: Michigan State University Press, 1958), p. 7.
5. Rosenman, *op. cit.,* p. 433.
6. Greer, *op. cit.,* pp. 4–5.

7. *Wartime Correspondence Between President Roosevelt and Pope Pius XII,* ed. Myron C. Taylor (New York: The Macmillan Co., 1947), p. 18.

8. *Ibid.,* p. 61.

9. Dietrich Bonhoeffer, *Ethics* (New York: The Macmillan Co., 1965), p. 356.

10. Eleanor Roosevelt, *This I Remember* (New York: Harper & Brothers, 1949), p. 341.

11. *Ibid.,* pp. 346–347.

12. Hartz, *The Liberal Tradition in America,* p. 263.

13. Eleanor Roosevelt, *op. cit.,* pp. 347–348. See also, for understanding FDR, *The Public Papers and Addresses of Franklin D. Roosevelt,* several volumes (New York: The Macmillan Co.), and *F.D.R., His Personal Letters,* several volumes (New York: Duell, Sloan and Pearce).

14. *The New York Times,* June 3, 1971, p. 43.

15. Daniel Boorstin, *The Image: A Guide to Pseudo-Events in America* (New York: Harper & Row, 1964).

16. Paul B. Sheatley and Jacob J. Feldman, "A National Survey on Public Reactions and Behavior," *The Kennedy Assassination,* p. 169.

17. From evidence coming to light in the summer of 1971 it is clear that the same information gap existed with respect to Vice-President Hubert Humphrey. He was not informed of any plans in Vietnam respecting bombing and troop buildup although the entire matter had been set forth in 1964 in the Johnson administration. On June 15, 1971, Senator Humphrey flatly stated that he did not know of these plans or documents and obviously was not in the "need to know" category. Such folly ignored history and the Truman experience. Of all Presidents, LBJ should have known better.

18. Harry Truman, *Memoirs: Years of Decision,* Vol. I (Garden City, N.Y.: Doubleday & Co., 1955), p. 419.

19. *Ibid.*

20. "America's Atomic Atrocity," *The Christian Century Reader,* ed. Harold E. Fey and Margaret Frakes (New York: Association Press, 1962), p. 263.

21. Harry Truman, *Memoirs: Years of Trial and Hope,* Vol. II (Garden City, N.Y.: Doubleday & Co., 1956), pp. 226–229.

22. *Ibid.,* p. 229.

23. Morison, *op. cit.,* p. 1069.

24. "The Truman Doctrine and America's Future," editorial, *The Christian Century,* Vol. 64, No. 16 (April 16, 1947), p. 483.

25. Amaury de Riencourt, *The American Empire* (New York: Dell Publishing Co., 1970), p. 92.

26. John Sutherland Bonnell, *Presidential Profiles: Religion in the Life of American Presidents* (Philadelphia: The Westminster Press, 1971), p. 215. It appears that Bonnell has misread the Truman *Memoirs.* Mr. Truman did say he attended church regularly as a boy, and Bonnell erroneously cites this as evidence to prove Truman did the same as an adult.

27. "Mr. Truman Attends Sunday School," editorial, *The Christian Century,* Vol. 64, No. 42 (October 15, 1947), p. 1228.

28. "Truman Calls Sermon on Mount Our Guide," editorial, *The Christian Century,* Vol. 66, No. 38 (September 21, 1949), p. 1091.

29. "Mr. Truman's Spiritual Blindness," editorial, *The Christian Century,* Vol. 67, No. 26 (June 28, 1950), p. 782.

30. *Public Papers of the President of the United States: Harry S. Truman—1952* (Washington: U.S. Government Printing Office, 1966), p. 1063.

31. *Public Papers of the President of the United States: Harry S. Truman—1951* (Washington: U.S. Government Printing Office, 1966), pp. 210, 548–549.

32. Hartz, *The Liberal Tradition in America,* p. 133.

33. Hoover, *American Road, 1933–1938,* p. 235.

34. Will Herberg, "Religion and Culture in Present-Day America," *The Record of American History,* Vol. II, ed. Irwin Unger, David Brody, and Paul Goodman (Waltham, Mass.: Xerox College Publishing, 1971), p. 448.

35. *Ibid.,* p. 453.

36. Baltzell, *op. cit.,* p. 296.

37. Herberg, *op. cit.,* p. 450.

38. Russell, *op. cit.,* p. xv.

39. Paul Hutchinson, "The President's Religious Faith," *The Christian Century,* Vol. 71, No. 12 (March 24, 1954), p. 362.

40. "The President Believes," editorial, *The Christian Century,* Vol. 75, No. 46 (November 12, 1958), p. 1294.

41. William G. McLoughlin, Jr., *Billy Graham: Revivalist in a Secular Age* (New York: The Ronald Press Co., 1960), p. 117.

42. "John Foster Dulles," editorial, *The Christian Century,* Vol. 72, No. 22 (June 1, 1955), p. 648.

43. Charles C. West, *Communism and the Theologians* (Philadelphia: The Westminster Press, 1958), p. 40.

44. *Ibid.,* p. 41.

45. Brinton, *op. cit.,* pp. 43–44.

46. Morison, *op. cit.,* p. 1079.

47. See William L. Miller, *Piety Along the Potomac: Notes on Politics and Morals in the Fifties* (Boston: Houghton Mifflin Co., 1964).

CHAPTER V

1. Richard M. Nixon, *Six Crises* (Garden City, N.Y.: Doubleday & Co., 1962), p. 412.

2. Pierre Berton, *The Comfortable Pew* (New York: J. B. Lippincott Co., 1965).

3. Merlin Gustafson, "The Religion of a President," *The Christian Century,* Vol. 86, No. 18 (April 30, 1969), p. 613.

4. "John F. Kennedy: An Overseas View," reprinted from *Economist,* in *The Christian Century,* Vol. 77, No. 3 (January 20, 1960), p. 76.

5. Harvey Cox, *The Secular City* (New York: The Macmillan Co., 1965), p. 63.

6. Theodore Sorenson, *Kennedy* (New York: Harper & Row, 1965), p. 19.

7. Baltzell, *op. cit.,* p. 270.

8. Andrew M. Greeley, *The Catholic Experience* (Garden City, N.Y.: Doubleday & Co., 1967), p. 288.

9. Eugene McCarthy, *The Limits of Power* (New York: Dell Publishing Co., 1968), p. 29.

10. *Public Papers of the President of the United States: John F. Kennedy—1963* (Washington: U.S. Government Printing Office, 1964), p. 336.

11. Greeley, *op. cit.,* p. 289.

12. Sorenson, *op. cit.,* p. 19.
13. Tom Wicker, *JFK and LBJ: The Influence of Personality upon Politics* (New York: William Morrow & Co., 1968), p. 124.
14. Eric F. Goldman, *The Tragedy of Lyndon Johnson* (New York: Alfred A. Knopf, 1969), p. 500.
15. J. William Fulbright, *The Arrogance of Power* (New York: Random House, 1966), p. 14.
16. John F. Kennedy, *Profiles in Courage* (New York: Harper & Brothers, 1956), p. 246.
17. *Ibid.,* pp. 238–239.
18. *Public Papers of the President of the United States: John F. Kennedy—1961* (Washington: U.S. Government Printing Office, 1962), p. 77.
19. *Ibid., 1962,* March 1, 1962.
20. Greeley, *op. cit.,* p. 291.
21. Goldman, *op. cit.,* p. 379.
22. Edwin S. Gaustad, *Historical Atlas of Religion in America* (New York: Harper & Row, 1962).
23. *Public Papers of the President of the United States: Lyndon B. Johnson—1964* (Washington: U.S. Government Printing Office, 1965).
24. For offering considerable insight into Mr. Johnson's administration I am indebted to Professor Eric Goldman of Princeton University who kindly consented to an interview on June 10, 1971.
25. Lady Bird Johnson, *A White House Diary* (New York: Holt, Rinehart & Winston, 1970).
26. James Reston, *Sketches in the Sand* (New York: Alfred A. Knopf, 1967), p. 393.
27. *Ibid.,* p. 392.
28. *The New York Times,* June 13, 1971.
29. "Notes from the News," *The Christian Century,* Vol. 85, No. 30 (July 24, 1968), p. 937.
30. Billy Graham, *Peace with God* (New York: Pocket Books, 1965), p. 238.
31. Nixon, *op. cit.,* p. 290.
32. Richard M. Nixon, "Asia After Viet Nam," *Foreign Affairs,* Vol. 46, No. 1 (October 1967), p. 123.
33. John C. Bennett, *Christianity and Communism Today* (New York: Association Press, 1970), p. 4.
34. Reinhold Niebuhr, "The President's Error," *Christianity and Crisis,* Vol. XXIX, No. 15 (September 15, 1969), pp. 227–228.
35. Garry Wills, *Nixon Agonistes* (Boston: Houghton Mifflin Co., 1970), p. 427.
36. *Ibid.*
37. Bonnell, *op. cit.*
38. *Ibid.,* p. 14.
39. *Public Papers of the President of the United States: Richard M. Nixon—1969* (Washington: U.S. Government Printing Office, 1970), p. 31.
40. *The New York Times,* March 10, 1971, p. 14.
41. "Quaker Meeting Criticizes Nixon," *The Christian Century,* Vol. 88, No. 16 (April 21, 1971), p. 488.
42. Wills, *op. cit.,* p. 182.

43. Reinhold Niebuhr, "The King's Chapel and the King's Court," *Christianity and Crisis,* Vol. XXIX, No. 14 (August 4, 1969), p. 211.

44. *Ibid.,* p. 212.

CHAPTER VI

1. Koenig, *op. cit.,* p. 304.
2. Morison, *op. cit.,* p. 846.
3. Norman Cousins, *Who Speaks for Man?* (New York: The Macmillan Co., 1953).
4. Morison, *op. cit.,* pp. 933–934.
5. Koenig, *op. cit.,* p. 318.
6. Morison, *op. cit.,* p. 917.
7. Baltzell, *op. cit.,* p. 231.
8. Truman, *Memoirs,* Vol. II, p. 271.
9. Wills, *op. cit.,* p. 127.
10. Koenig, *op. cit.,* p. 301.
11. Rexford Tugwell, "The Historians and the Presidency," *Political Science Quarterly,* Vol. LXXXVI, No. 2 (June 1971), p. 194.
12. Wicker, *op. cit.,* p. 148.
13. Many of the ideas presented here about LBJ were inspired by an interview with Eric Goldman.
14. Tugwell, *op. cit.*

CHAPTER VII

1. Bonhoeffer, *op. cit.,* p. 105.
2. Hartz, "Revolution," p. 133.
3. John F. Wilson, *op. cit.,* p. 20.
4. E. E. Evans-Pritchard, *Theories of Primitive Religion* (Oxford: The Clarendon Press, 1965), p. 64.
5. Emil Durkheim, *The Elementary Forms of the Religious Life* (London: George Allen & Unwin, 1968), p. 47.
6. *Ibid.,* p. 446.
7. Conrad Cherry, ed., *God's New Israel: Religious Interpretations of American Destiny* (Englewood Cliffs, N.J.: Prentice-Hall, 1971), pp. 1–24.
8. West, *op. cit.,* p. 43.
9. Reston, *Sketches,* p. 470.
10. Bellah, *op. cit.,* p. 18.
11. *Ibid.,* p. 14.
12. Wills, *op. cit.,* p. 480.
13. *Ibid.,* p. 564.
14. *Ibid.,* p. 547.
15. *Ibid.,* p. 480.
16. Goldman, *Tragedy,* pp. 385–386.
17. Brinton, *op. cit.,* p. 19.
18. Wills, *op. cit.,* p. 433. An excellent study of the entire problem is Kenneth W. Thompson, *Christian Ethics and the Dilemmas of Foreign Policy* (Durham, N.C.: Duke University Press, 1959).
19. Henry Steele Commager, "The Roots of Lawlessness," *Saturday Review,* Vol. LIV, No. 7 (February 13, 1971), p. 64.